UP AGAINST THE
CLOCK

UP AGAINST THE
CL⊙CK

How You Can Double Your Time?

A MANAGER'S GUIDE FOR THOSE WHO DON'T HAVE TIME TO READ TIME MANAGEMENT BOOKS

RONALD C. MENDLIN

REGENT PRESS
Berkeley, California

ISBN 13: 978-1-58790-153-9
ISBN 10: 1-58790-153-6
Library of Congress Control Number: 2008924839

REGENT PRESS
2747 Regent Street
Berkeley, CA 94705
www.regentpress.net
ph: 510-845-1196
fax: 510-704-1543
regentpress@mindspring.com

ACKNOWLEDGEMENTS

I would like to express heartfelt appreciation to
Milt Reiterman,
Barry Newborn,
and Shirley Melnicoe,
who have contributed, in their own words,
practiced insight and managerial wisdom
to this work.

I should like to thank John Schofield,
former C.E.O. of A.F.C. (mid-cap company)
for reviewing this book.

I would also like to thank my wife,
Lorraine Mendlin,
for her invaluable support and encouragement
with this project and in all things.

Finally, thank you to Jist WORKS, Inc.
for allowing me to excerpt much of the material
included in Chapter 8, "Unstressing."

REGENT PRESS

CONTACT: Mark Weiman

2747 Regent Street
Berkeley, CA 94705
Phone: 510-845-1196
Fax: 510-704-1543
regentpress@mindspring.com
www.regentpress.net

FOR FAVOR OF REVIEW

TITLE:

UP AGAINST THE CLOCK
How You Can Double Your Time?
*A Manager's Guide For Those Who Don't Have Time
To Read Time Management Books*

AUTHOR	Ronald C. Mendlin
PUB. DATE:	January 1, 2009 / NOW AVAILABLE!
PRICE:	$19.95
ISBN-13:	978-1-58790-153-9
PAGES:	184 pages / paperback / 5.5" x 8.5"
SUBJECT:	Business / Management / Motivation

ABOUT THE BOOK: *Up Against The Clock* covers the essential gamut of time management wisdom, and provides useful information about attitude and self-evaluation, organizing a clear and streamlined workspace,

"greasing the wheels" of an optimally efficient work environment. The book's purpose is to effectively double your time efficiency with tested and proven time-saving methods that apply to a variety of day-to-day situations. If the ideas presented in this book are practiced diligently, they will lead to success both on and off the job. *Up Against The Clock* can be used as a handy reference manual or a primer to be read straight through. It is also a workbook, with written exercises to be filled in and completed.

ABOUT THE AUTHOR: RONALD C. MENDLIN has over 40 years experience in 14 different business fields. He has reorganized sections of several San Francisco City Departments, including the Board of Education, the Tax Collector's Office, the Department of Public Health and the S.F. Airport Commission. He has also saved the S.F. Municipal Railway from financial embarrassment. In his 30 years with the City and County of San Francisco, Ronald Mendlin was the recipient of numerous written commendations from mayors and various government administrators for leadership of projects and superior job performance. Working on a part-time basis at the Northern California Service League, he was credited by the California Department of Corrections' Jobs Plus Program for assisting over 750 ex-felons in getting jobs. He is also the co-author of the *Putting The Bars Behind You Series* which, in a five-year period, has sold over 40,000 copies throughout the U.S.

■ Table of Contents

Don't Be Afraid To Purge. Nuggets Of Efficiency. Write Your Own Rules.

■ Preface

For managers and small business owners, effective time management is not an abstract consideration. On the contrary, time management skills can be the difference between keeping a job and losing one, staying in business or closing up shop, frustration or fulfillment.

Because managers are responsible for managing others people's time as well as their own, the impact of bad or good time management is immediately evident for them, every day.

I feel that the time has come for a book on time management that is written with managers in mind, does not waste the reader's time, and marries inspiration with pragmatism. The book you are holding in your hands is the product of nearly four decades of management experience in numerous fields. It contains the distilled knowledge of many time management experts as well as my own experience and that of the managers whom I interviewed for this project.

UP AGAINST THE CLOCK: A MANAGER'S GUIDE TO TIME MANAGEMENT covers the essential gamut of time management wisdom, and provides useful information about attitude and self-evaluation, organizing a clear and streamlined workspace, running effective meetings, getting the best out of employees, and generally "greasing the wheels" of an optimally efficient work environment. One of my hopes for this book is that you might benefit from some of my own early mistakes.

The book's purpose is to effectively double your time efficiency with tested and proven time-saving methods that apply to a variety of day-to-day situations. If the ideas presented in this book are practiced diligently, they will lead to success both on and off the job, including the achievement of overarching life goals.

You can use this book as a handy reference manual, a primer to be read straight through from start to finish, or both. It is also a workbook. As efficiency is a hallmark of time management, I have strived to be concise, and to keep the table of contents straightforward and simple. I think you will find it easy to adapt this book to your needs.

■ How To Use This Book

The time-saving techniques in this book will:

■ **Afford you new opportunities to be successful at your job.**

■ **Allow you to lead a more balanced life.**

■ **Give you more spare time in which to channel your energies in different positive directions.**

This book is for people who take time management seriously, and know that they *need* to take it seriously. Consider this book an amicable companion. If you like, read it cover to cover, but if it suits you instead to treat it as a reference guide, by all means please do. Many of the ideas in this book are universally applicable, but not all of them will fit your particular situation. Take what you find useful and adapt it to your needs.

Throughout the book you'll be prompted to do a number of written exercises, and to make various lists. The interactive assignments in this book are intended to help "concretize" the book's ideas and, occasionally, to jog your creativity. Cognitive research has conclusively demonstrated that writing things down helps to sharpen thinking and illuminate issues at hand. I believe you will derive maximum benefit from this book if you take the time to do all or most of the exercises. (The last thing I would ever do is *waste* your time with useless busy work!) You may even want to repeat some of the exercises in six months or a year, depending on how valuable they prove for you, and if they lead to any useful changes in your work habits.

I also have a "secret agenda": I hope that the concepts in this book will do more than improve your work efficiency; I hope they will ultimately provide you with enhanced fulfillment in your life. When you put down this book, I want you to be happier than you were before you picked it up. If that sounds overly ambitious (or, forgive me, grandiose) for a book on time management for managers, consider again that time is our most precious currency. How much is an hour worth? Or a day? Regardless of your hourly or yearly salary, the truest answer is that each day and each hour is priceless, and scarcely anything in this world will make you happier than the knowledge that you are putting your time to good use, that you are using your days and your hours well, that you are in control of your time — insofar as control is desirable and possible.

Introduction

■ Your Life And Time

"The secret of success is constancy of purpose."

— DISRAELI

Time, time, time!!! Your success in life will largely be the result of how you organize and utilize your time.

There is so little of it, and yet we must make the most of it. It's our most precious resource, but so few of us know how to use it wisely. Too few people realize that their spare time can be many times more valuable than gold.

> **EVERYONE** gets 365 days a year, and 24 hours in each day which means that there are 1,440 minutes in a day, 168 hours in a week, and 8,760 hours in a year. If each week you work 40 hours, sleep 56 hours, eat for 21 hours, and devote 14 hours for recreation, you still have 37 hours to spare. What will you do with them?

Suppose you want to learn about a subject. If you spend 20 hours researching or studying, you'll know more about that subject than most people. It's also been said that if you spend one hour each day learning about a given company, you could be president of that company in five years' time. So, simply put, today is yesterday's plans put into action.

This book contains guidelines for using time well. With over 35 years of involvement with management and training I believe I have learned some things, and I want to tell you about them (though the telling will not take over 35 years!).

 **A BALANCING ACT**

"It isn't changing around from place to place that keeps you lively. It's getting time on your side. Working with it, not against it."

– URSULA LE GUIN (FROM *THE DISPOSSESSED*)

What does it mean to "get time on your side"? Getting time on your side involves striking a dynamic balance. Time is precious and limited, but it serves little purpose to become obsessive about it. As a general rule, you should not put off until tomorrow what you can accomplish today, but it is equally important not to try and cram every possible thing into an hour or a day. You need breathing space. Eating well and getting proper sleep are absolutely essential to making the best use of your time, but you can also take advantage of insomnia once in a while to get a few things done.

Ultimately, the key ingredients of effective time management are *attitude* and *organization* and *analyzing*. Everything in this book proceeds from these three principles.

 **ANALYZING**

You set up an organizational system that can save time, money and energy. You have the right attitude, and it does not work. Your next step is to analyze why it did not work. Note: So many people analyze a problem to death. Use a moderate amount of thinking, try something. It is easier when you get feedback.

A STREAMLINED ATTITUDE

Debra, who has owned and managed a successful restaurant for over a decade, used to be at odds with time. Now she works *with* time, not against it. "I used to imagine that eventually, if I crossed enough items off of my to-do list, I'd be finished, and then I'd get to relax. But now I've realized there's no such thing as 'getting it all done.' At least not until I'm dead!"

"I used to be in a constant state of panic because I could never *finish*. But I've come to accept that the list never ends. If I just keep doing things at a reasonable pace, though, it's all going to be okay. And that's the important thing." Debra understands that in mastering her *attitude*, she is able to "enjoy the ride" with time.

"You're always on a learning curve. Not only is your list never done, but you will never arrive at being good enough, fast enough, smart enough, and that's a good thing! That's not a bad thing, as long as you're always getting a little better, and you can see what you've learned. I don't think anyone really gets to the place where they can say, 'Now I'm a good manager and I know all the tricks.'"

"Life is like rapids. There are moments where you stop and say 'Hmm, that was good,' and you enjoy those moments, but there's always another rapid coming. It's always something, whether it's your personal life, or the business climate, or your own job skills, or politics, or the weather. It's always something. The process itself is it, is life. There is no arrival." Debra understands that a good relationship with time is grounded in acceptance, not just of time, but of herself.

Sometimes you will make mistakes. As the saying goes, "He who never makes a mistake never makes anything." But never punish yourself. Forgive yourself quickly for your mistakes. (They were, after all, mistakes.) Above all, don't let the past become a burden. What's done is done. Don't get mired in regrets or guilt. You can't change the past, but your choices in the present will sow the seeds of the future. Give yourself credit for everything you learn, and for all you accomplish. Be good to yourself, and to those around you. Believe it or not, these are all important principles of time management.

Chapter 1

■ Your Office Space: The Ecology Of Efficiency

"For the most part, we, who could choose simplicity, choose complication."

— ANNE MORROW LINDBERGH, *GIFT FROM THE SEA*

Managing your time starts with examining how you manage your space. Space management is more than simply knowing where everything is in your office. Space management is about creating the optimal environment for you to feel at ease and to work efficiently. Creating an ecology (or environment) of efficiency begins with the principles described in this chapter.

■ YOUR DESK

Start with where you live. Your desk, in a sense, is your home, your touchstone, your base of operations. Some might even say your desk is a reflection of your state of mind.

Chances are you spend a significant amount of time at your desk. So your desk should be organized in a way that compliments your rhythm and style of work.

Almost everyone works better at an uncluttered desk. Even if you're a creative genius, it does little good to have random piles of paper that you have to sort through whenever you're looking for a particular document, or to have multiple files and projects open at the same time.

Keep it simple. If there's something for you to sign, sign it immediately and be rid of it. If there's something to file, file it immediately or, at the very least, place it in a designated To Be Filed pile.

FIRST RULE OF THE DESKTOP: *Only keep on your desk those items that you need easy access to today, or that you use on a regular basis.*

Second Rule of the Desktop: *Keep closest to you those items that you use the most frequently.*

 DECLUTTERING

Think about it. For each of the items listed below, assign a value of "1" if it's something you reach for several times a day, "2" if you reach for it once or twice a day, "3" if you reach for it less than once a day, and "4" if you reach for it less than once a week.

___ stapler

___ pens/pencils

___ paper clips

___ scotch tape

___ glue stick

___ calculator

___ staple remover

___ correction fluid

___ pencils

___ blank floppy or zip disks or CDs

___ writing pad

___ stationery

___ blank forms

___ datebook

___ highlighter

___ personal address/phone book or rolodex

___ dictation tape recorder

___ markers

___ sticky notepads

___ scissors

___ reference books

___ information sheets

___ _____

___ _____

___ _____

___ _____

___ _____

Items identified as "3" or "4" really don't belong on your desk. They can live just as happily on a shelf.

Although it is advisable to clear off your desk each day before you go home (and perhaps before lunch as well), some people like to leave themselves a small to-do list of tasks for when they arrive the next day. They find that this list "jump starts" their thinking and organizing processes in the morning. If this works for you, do it.

Of course you may also want to keep personal items on your desk, such as photographs, or other sentimental items. Your desk is a kind of home, after all. It's a very personal space. So by all means, give your desk a welcoming character. But don't collect knickknacks that just get in your way.

PAPERS, PAPERS, PAPERS!

It's all well and good to say you should keep your desk clear, but you are probably deluged with memos, letters, bills, brochures, and documents of all sorts in your inbox every day.

There are four things you can do with any given piece of paper:

1 **Deal with it immediately and be done with it. (This includes delegating it to someone else).**

2 **Categorize it into a pile to be dealt with sometime later.**

3 **File it away off your desk.**

4 **Toss it into the nearest recycling bin.**

The only other possibility is to leave the paper sitting randomly somewhere on your desk, and I do not recommend that.

 EMAILS AND ELECTRONIC FILES

Treat your electronic files and emails similarly to how you treat all of the hard copy that you encounter. The principles of sorting in this chapter are as applicable to computer files and emails as they are to paper.

It's very easy to let messages pile up in your email inbox. What's the harm? They don't really take up space, do they? Well, actually they do. They take up space in your computer's memory but more importantly, emails that never get deleted can create clutter in your mind. "Have I read that email? Do I need to reread that email?" As your email inbox grows, so grows an insidious sense of encroaching chaos.

Your emails and electronic files must either be filed into their proper folders, or deleted. Files should not loiter on your computer desktop, and emails should be purged from your inbox on a regular basis.

■ THE BIG SORT

It is inevitable that papers will sometimes pile up in your inbox or on your desktop. At least every day or two, you have to attack that stack.

When you go into attack mode, you must look at one item at a time and decide *immediately* what you will do with each piece of paper. Do not make an "undecided" pile. An "undecided" pile is just another thing you will have to deal with later.

One popular method of sorting your stack into coherent piles is to designate each document either:

■ **TOP PRIORITY:** immediate action required.

■ **MEDIUM PRIORITY:** action required some time in the next few days.

■ **LOW PRIORITY:** no specific action required in the immediate future; to be filed or read when you have time.

■ **NO PRIORITY:** recycle bin bound.

WORK AS YOU'RE SORTING

As you are plowing through your stack, if you come across memos or letters that require a short to-the-point response, answer them immediately. Don't even bother putting them in the A pile; just dispatch them right away. It's usually easier to dash off a reply in the moment when the issue is fresh in your mind than it will be later when you would have to reexamine the document.

If you need more time to formulate a response, then make a few notes to yourself on the document or on an attached note before moving the document. That way, when you get to it later, you'll have a reminder of what you want to say, and the process will go much quicker.

Put stray business cards immediately into your organizer or take a minute to record the information into your hard-copy or computer address book. Unless you have a system to organize business cards, it's probably best not to collect business cards.

If it's not immediately clear what to do with a given piece of paper, try asking yourself the following questions.

■ **Is this something I can take care of right here and now? (If yes: do it).**

■ **What would happen if I lost this document? Could I live without it? (If yes: recycle bin).**

■ **Do I have this information in another form somewhere else? (If so: recycle bin).**

■ **Is this something I'll need easy access to today or tomorrow? (If not: file).**

■ **If I were going on vacation in a few days, what would I do with this document? (Do that).**

Make your life easier by getting rid of as much paper as possible including unneeded copies of documents (never make more copies than you need!), outdated reference materials, catalogs you'll never get around to opening, and general information that doesn't pertain to your particular job. Send these to be recycled, and then get back to your sorting.

■ TYPES OF PILES

If you must keep piles of papers on your desk, know which piles are which and keep them organized and consistent. Don't move them around; you'll only confuse yourself. Consider the types of documents that tend to reside on your desktop. How many piles do you truly need?

■ KNOW YOUR PILES

The following are examples of piles that some people have on their desks. If you keep additional types of piles, name them in the blank spaces following:

- **To-be-filed pile.**
- **To-be-read pile.**
- **To-be-completed today pile.**

_____

_____

_____

_____

Just remember: The fewer piles the better!

LISTS

Debra: "During the course of a day, I'll think of things to do, and I shove little notes in my pocket all day long. At the end of the day, I go through my pockets. A lot of stuff that seemed important when it occurred to me gets thrown away, but a few things go on my to-do list for the next day."

Lists can be helpful—I recommend them for particular uses and depending on your style and needs. It's important to work with lists in a way that proves useful to you over time. For example, some authorities discourage the accumulation of list-like notes on small scraps of paper, but Debra is on her feet most of the day, so the "scraps method" works for her.

One of the downsides of lists is that you can wind up with too many of them if you're not careful, especially if you don't regularly throw away, combine, or update your lists. You could even wind up with a pile of lists on your desk! Make sure you don't overload any particular list. You don't want to feel overwhelmed by the sight of any list.

Milt Reiterman, who served as Deputy Superintendent of the San Francisco Unified School District, says, "I keep meticulous lists. But a list is only as good as it can actually serve you in relationship to meeting your objectives. Your list shouldn't dictate things to you, because sometimes you have to drop things off the list. A list is only one factor in time management; a list is not an end in itself."

LETTING GO OF LISTS

List making is an ongoing activity. Which of the following types of lists on the facing page do you keep? Which should you keep that you currently do not? Which ones could you let go of?

Lists are an oddly personal organizing tool. It is unlikely that any two people, even if they hold identical jobs, should be keeping the exact same lists. However, what is universally true is that lists should be constantly updated because lists, like newspapers, become outdated quickly.

USED	TYPE OF LIST	REASONS FOR STARTING OR STOPPING USING LIST (E.G. HELPS ME REMEMBER, DON'T REALLY NEED, ETC.).
	Daily to-do list	
	List of thngs to accomplish before lunch, or in the next hour	
	Checklist of small steps required to accomplish a routine task	
	List of people to call	
	Monthly goals list	
	Yearly goals list	
	List of tasks or projects ranked in order of priority or due date	
	Major project list	

■ CALENDARS

Calendars are another outstanding organizational tool and are somewhat more fixed than lists. You can keep a wall calendar or a pocket appointment calendar, or both, depending on what suits you. Some people also find it useful to keep a personal calendar at home, on which to record planned activities for the family. Unless you have an extraordinary memory, you probably need at least one calendar in your life. Things to note on your calendar include:

- **Business appointments**
- **Personal appointments**
- **Doctor and dental appointments**
- **Phone numbers of the people with whom you have appointments**
- **Deadlines**
- **Planned activities**
- **Meeting dates and times**
- **Reminders to follow up on contacts or projects**

In selecting a portable appointment calendar, make sure that it gives you enough space to write all you need, that it's easy to carry, and that it shows you at a glance what you need to see—be it each day, week, or month.

■ FILING SYSTEM

A good filing system is a joy, because it allows you to know exactly where to find what you need when you need it. But a filing system cannot be as personal as a list or calendar, because other people may also need to access your files, either now or in the future.

The following simple principles can help to streamline just about any filing system.

■ Whenever you file something that is related to an action you must take in the future, make a note about it on one of your to-do lists immediately, so that it doesn't become a casualty of "out of sight, out of mind."

■ Give your files specific descriptive names. If you have several documents that you cannot easily categorize, and you think you may need them in the near future, a miscellaneous temporary folder can be useful. But don't let documents "live" in this folder for long; categorize and file them as quickly as possible, and don't let this folder expand to more than ten documents.

■ Before putting a document in a file, first ask yourself: What general subject is most likely to come to your mind? When you go back to look for that document, make sure it is filed under the general subject that comes to your mind.

■ In your file drawers, don't place your file tabs directly behind each other. Stagger them from left to right for better visibility.

■ Better yet, have open file shelves (or "vertical files") in your office for your most-used files, keeping the file folders in a vertical position so that they're easy to see and access.

■ Generally speaking, it's better to have fewer, fatter files than many tiny ones. This makes it much easier to remember where you filed any given document. However, if files become huge or unwieldy, you should divide them.

■ Purge your files of outdated or unneeded documents on a regular basis. Send historical documents to an archive. Toss the others. Most data has a "shelf life" of no more than five years.

■ If you've inherited files that reside in your drawers, but which you yourself do not need, get them out of your personal work space. Send them to an archive, or just put them in the recycle bin if no one will ever need them.

■ Always place the most recent documents at the front of your files.

■ Unfold papers before you file them.

■ Don't put envelopes into your file folders; they take up unnecessary space.

■ Always keep extra file folders handy, but not on your desktop!

■ TYPES OF FILES

The following are a few common types of files you might keep:

■ **Specific work project files**

■ **Specific client or customer files**

■ **Budgets**

■ **Meeting minutes**

■ **Temporary files**

One manager keeps a purple file of little things that have to get done, like taxes, letters to be mailed, or an audit that needs to be sent out to somebody.

RETHINKING YOUR FILES

What other types of files do you have?

_____

_____

_____

_____

_____

Do you have any thin files that you might be able to eliminate or combine with others? If so, which ones?

_____

_____

_____

_____

_____

Do you have any files that you haven't needed to access for several months, which could possibly be eliminated or moved to archives? If so, which ones?

_____

_____

_____

_____

_____

_____

_____

_____

Your filing system should be manageable and simple. It should not be chaotic or overcrowded. Your filing system is a foundational element of your work environment and you should feel completely comfortable with it. Smooth information retrieval affords you a sense of ease and control.

A WORD ABOUT FORMS

Occasionally, you may find yourself working with a standard company form that documents information you don't really need, or information that's duplicated elsewhere. Perhaps this form could be combined with another existing form, or even eliminated.

Minimizing paperwork saves time and energy. A lot of forms generate more work than they save. Be on the lookout for unnecessary reports and forms, and cull them from your workspace.

If you don't have the authority to do away with an unnecessary form or reporting mechanism, tell someone who does have the authority why eliminating this superfluous paperwork could benefit your organization by improving efficiency.

READING MATERIAL

There are things to do, and then there are things to read. But sometimes the distinction is not clear. Many of the papers that cross your desk have to be read and thus they become things to do.

But what about the blizzard of brochures, announcements, company memos, newspapers, magazines, catalogs, and (yes) books that buries you continually, at work and at home? How do you decide what to actually read, and when? And where do you put all of it? Begin by really examining your schedule and deciding how much time you have to read each week. How many hours a week do you have for reading, and how many of those hours do you want to spend reading periodicals? How many periodicals can you realistically fit into that time frame?

■ SETTING YOUR READING PRIORITIES

Start with magazines, professional journals, newsletters, and any other periodicals that you are currently subscribed to. Make a list of all of them:

Rank   Name

___   _____

___   _____

___   _____

_____ _____

_____ _____

_____ _____

_____ _____

_____ _____

_____ _____

_____ _____

_____ _____

Assign a "1" rank if you regularly find information in it that is useful for your work and/or your personal life. Also, write a "1" if you regularly read and enjoy it. Assign a "2" rank if this publication occasionally gives you useful information, or you occasionally enjoy it. Assign a "3" if you rarely or never have time to read it.

Toss every periodical that did not get either a "1" or a "2." Either cancel your subscription, or pass it on to someone else (preferably someone who can derive value from it) as soon as it comes. You might also want to dump some of your "2"s.

You need to be ruthless about this; otherwise, your stack of unread reading materials will only make you feel guilty. This is not efficient! Don't fall into the trap of being an information collector. Just because something *looks* interesting or useful doesn't mean that you should try to read it — especially if it's been stagnating in your "To Read" pile for months.

You have your limits. You can not do, or read, everything, even if it is (possibly) worth reading. The best policy is to rid yourself of all the reading material that you don't get around to after 2 months. If you can not bring yourself to do that, or if you're afraid that you *might* need all these materials some day, you should go ahead and create a file called "Unread Reading Material." You still won't get around to reading it, but at least it will be off your desk, so it probably won't bother you as much. In fact, you'll probably forget it's even there.

■ SKIMMING

Depending on what you're reading, you may want to skim or scan for relevant information rather than pouring over every word. Often, you do not really know whether or not you need to read something until you skim.

To skim, find a conclusion or a summary section before delving into the body of the document. Read first sentences of paragraphs. Highlight points that may be useful for your purposes. Or, better yet, if you can, have an administrative assistant review the document for pertinent information, and then give it to you pre-highlighted. Of course, you'll need to carefully explain to your assistant the type of information you're interested in, so that he or she can competently perform this task for you.

A note of caution: *Skim reading* is not the same thing as *rush reading*. If you try to rush through your reading material, you probably won't retain or comprehend most of what you've read. Think of *skimming* as touching the surface lightly like a stone across a brook, rather than as skipping ahead.

■ WHEN TO READ

The best time to read non-urgent information is during a relatively relaxed, low-energy part of your day, perhaps while you're waiting for a bus or commuter train. But if it's something very brief, like an announcement or a short memo, read it immediately. It may have time-sensitive information that you need to keep in mind. After you read it, get rid of the document itself, unless it contains a lot of information that you can't easily jot down.

For many people, it is helpful to designate a certain time of day for reading. Some managers budget at least 30 minutes per day for reading.

■ AFTER READING

Create files of reference materials that contain information you might need again, after you have read the information and have identified useful passages. When there is only one or two useful sections, either highlight those sections, flag or paper clip them, copy the relevant pages, or cut them out rather than filing the whole magazine, newsletter, or journal.

Brochures and catalogs may also be useful to keep on file — for a limited time.

DON'T BE AFRAID TO PURGE

Have a look at your "To Be Read" materials.

Make a list of all the materials you've been "planning" to read for over a month. Ask yourself which ones you really need to read, and which ones you could probably live without reading. Make an X next to those you could let go of without sacrificing any significant edification or gratification. If you're unsure, put down a '?'.

_____ _____

_____ _____

_____ _____

_____ _____

_____ _____

_____ _____

_____ _____

_____ _____

_____ _____

NUGGETS OF EFFICIENCY

Here are a few principles for an efficient work environment:

- Clearly label all your binders and folders.

- Generate as little paperwork as you possibly can. For example, don't make unnecessary copies, and don't write a memo when a short email will work just as well.

- Organize your bookshelf into sections.

- Keep an adequate supply on hand of the items you need and use the most.

- Avoid clutter by not buying things you don't need. If you have one of something already, don't get a second one unless you really need two, or the first one requires replacement. When you add a new item, remove an old one.

■ WRITE YOUR OWN RULES

Can you think of any workplace organizing principles that are particular to your working environment? Write them in the spaces below and in the spaces on the following page.

_____

_____

_____

_____

_____

_____

_____

_____

_____

Chapter 2

Getting Things Done

"Men acquire a particular quality by constantly acting a particular way . . . you become just by performing just actions, temperate by performing temperate actions, brave by performing brave actions."

— ARISTOTLE

"Step by step the job is done."

— UNKNOWN

ESSENTIAL EFFICIENCY

Efficiency is using time to its greatest effect. Being efficient doesn't necessarily mean that you get everything done, but it means that you do accomplish the most important things.

FIRST RULE OF EFFICIENCY:
Know what is important.

SECOND RULE OF EFFICIENCY: *Continually reorient yourself to the important things.*

Figuring out what's most important is also called **setting priorities.** Begin by answering the following questions:

- **What is my most important project at this time?**

- **What am I currently responsible for that will have the most impact on my company's long-term success?**

- **What is the best use of my time and energy right now?**

Staying on track with what's most important is tricky, because what is most important can change in the course of a single day. You have to remain focused and at the same time remain flexible. It is helpful to have clear goals for the day, month, or year. But even goals have to change.

As a general rule, important goals, tasks, and projects are those that have a major impact on your organization's long-term viability and success. These may include product development, market research, equipment upgrades, media campaigns, or employee training.

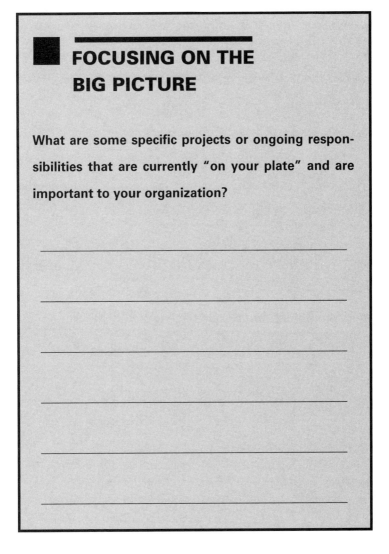

FOCUSING ON THE BIG PICTURE

What are some specific projects or ongoing responsibilities that are currently "on your plate" and are important to your organization?

■ OBSTACLES TO EFFECTIVE PRIORITIZING

Just because something grabs your attention doesn't necessarily make it important. Sometimes a task is done simply because it is right in front of your nose. Or sometimes you're tempted to complete the easiest tasks first, rather than tackling the more complex jobs.

Many managers often find themselves busy with matters of secondary importance, which they should rightfully delegate to someone else.

If one of your subordinates turns in work early, you may feel obligated to review it promptly even if its importance is not imminent. You should instead simply thank them for their timely work and then turn back to your priorities.

IDENTIFYING OBSTACLES

What is it that keeps you from focusing on your priorities? Check all that apply.

_____   Coworker-related distractions.

_____   Feeling overwhelmed in the face of complex, lengthy projects.

_____   Time-consuming routines, involving relatively trivial tasks.

_____   Excessive record keeping, filing, or copying.

_____   Lack of clarity.

_____   Bad relationships at work.

_____   _____

_____   _____

_____   _____

_____   _____

_____   _____

_____   _____

When you are aware of what's going on in your mind and your feelings, then the obstacles are easier to overcome. For example, if you notice that you're feeling restless and it is hard to concentrate on a challenging task, simply recognizing the restlessness can help. Then you can decide whether or not to forge ahead despite the restlessness, or to take a break and turn to some less demanding activity.

.

Honor your limits. Strike a balance between self-discipline and self-care. When you're feeling flustered or confused, come back to the simple questions. First what do I need to do? What tasks are most important? What can wait?

■ BREAK IT DOWN

It's such a well-known technique; it's almost a cliché. And it works, it works, it works. Break jobs down into easy, manageable subtasks. And if the smaller tasks are still a little daunting, break those down as well.

It's probably the most common reason that we procrastinate and avoid our major projects. They loom too large. We look at the big picture and we melt. But as Henry Ford once said, "Nothing is particularly hard if you divide it into small parts."

When you're confronted with a new job or project, make a blueprint for accomplishing it that includes specific steps. You can always alter your plan along the way; it is not set in stone. Some projects should be divided not just into steps, but also into smaller, separate projects. *Keep it manageable.* One step should lead to another, and another.

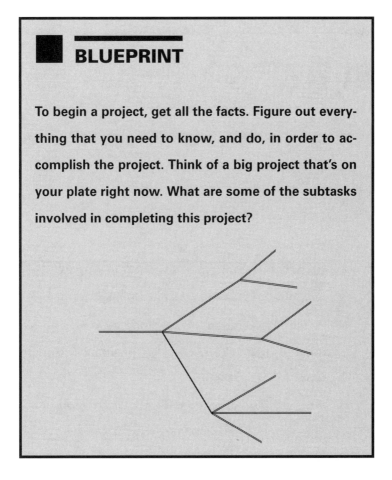

■ **BLUEPRINT**

To begin a project, get all the facts. Figure out everything that you need to know, and do, in order to accomplish the project. Think of a big project that's on your plate right now. What are some of the subtasks involved in completing this project?

You can break up almost any subtask into smaller parts that take no more than fifteen minutes. Break the subtasks you listed above into smaller tasks.

With particularly challenging or unpleasant projects, make a commitment to work on them 20 to 30 minutes a day. If you've broken them down well, you'll make observable progress quickly.

EXAMPLES

TASK: CREATE A NEW JOB DESCRIPTION FOR A NEW EMPLOYEE

Subtask 1: Prepare the job description document

- Write out a brief overview/job description
- Include primary duties responsibilities of the job
- Include description of key internal and external relationships inherent in the position, including reporting relationships
- If the position is brand new, give it an appropriate title

Subtask 2: **Review job description with employee**

■ Make sure the employee understands all aspects of the position and what the expectations are

■ Describe the basis on which the employee will be evaluated, based on the job description

■ Solicit questions from the employee regarding the job description

TASK: SETTING UP A MEETING

Subtask 1: **Personal preparation**

■ Create an agenda

■ Review all pertinent documentation

■ Review your goals for the meeting

Subtask 2: **Take care of meeting logistics**

■ Set meeting time and place

■ Communicate meeting time and place to attendees

■ Distribute agenda in advance to attendees

SETTING YOUR GOALS

Some work goals are handed down to you from above, or are dictated by the objectives of your company. However, even within the context of your company's larger goals, you must often set some goals and some timelines for yourself. As a manager, this is your creative responsibility. No one else can do it for you.

Begin by assessing the situation you're faced with and answering these questions:

■ **What are the most important desired outcomes (goals)?**

■ **What conditions will ensure or make likely these outcomes?**

■ **What can I do now to create these conditions, and to bring about these outcomes?**

The next step is to formulate a plan of action based on working backwards from your goals. What needs to occur immediately before the goal is accomplished? And before that? And before that?

In this way, you may come up with multiple avenues to your goals. Pick the avenue that seems most realistic and efficient, but as always, remain flexible.

■ PLAN OF ACTION

Write down one to three goals you want to accomplish in the next month.

1._____

2._____

3._____

Write down one to three goals you want to accomplish in the next year.

1. _____

2. _____

3. _____

Now for each goal, write down at least three conditions that will have to be met before that goal can be
accomplished.

Goal:

Condition 1_____

Condition 2 _____

Condition 3_____

For each of the conditions you have listed, write
down specific actions you can take to bring about
these conditions.

Goal 1:

Condition 1 _____

Action 1_____

Condition 2 _____

Action 2_____

Condition 3 _____

Action 3_____

> Continue until you have identified the actions you
> can take to bring about the right conditions to meet
> your goals.
>
> Spend at least one hour a week working on your
> year-end goals.

 THE TASK OF WRITING

A word or two needs to be said about tasks that involve writing. Many people dread having to write. There is something inherently intimidating about a blank page. But the fact is, when you break it down, writing is just like any other task.

When you have to write, for example, a report, begin by brainstorming all the things you need to say, all the points you have to cover. Just list these points at random on scratch paper. Then *rank* them, either chronologically (that is, according to which points must logically precede others so that your report makes sense), or in order of their relative importance to your topic. Based on these rankings, decide which points you will discuss first, second, third, and so on, paragraph by paragraph.

If you identify a point that seems like it may be difficult to articulate, break it into constituent parts. Maybe articulating the point will require an additional paragraph or two. (Sometimes you don't know until you start to actually write.)

The most important thing is to *start.* Writing, like anything else, won't get done until you do it. Unlike many other tasks, though, the prospect of having to write often gives rise to anxiety, even though many people find that the writing itself is often quite pleasant.

One manager approaches it this way: "When I have to write something, I'll do many drafts. I'll go wild with a piece that's going to end up being a page and a half, and it will be six pages long at first, and then I work on it 20, 30 times, a little at a time."

Another manager suggests the following method, "If you get stuck in your writing, write the problem or task at the top of a sheet of paper. Then let your subconscious take over. Write down whatever flows through your brain. If nothing comes at first, go for a walk and take your notebook with you. When I do that, solutions and ideas come to me out of nowhere, and I jot them down immediately."

■ SCHEDULING

Efficient scheduling is an important component of getting things done. Here are a few basic principles of common-sense scheduling:

- **Group related tasks together. Some meetings, memos, phone calls, etc. are related to the same subject or project. If you schedule them close to each other, they'll go quicker.**

- **Group your errands together. Schedule appointments close together in time and in geographical space.**

- **Check your calendar on a regular basis.**

- **In scheduling your time, honor your commitments to yourself just as you would honor the needs and priorities of others.**

EFFICIENT SCHEDULING

Imagine that you have at least three things you MUST get done today:

- **Finish writing a report.**

- **Talk to an employee about a problem situation.**

- **Catch up on your emails.**

In what order would you tackle these tasks and why?

_____

_____

_____

_____

_____

Schedule unpleasant tasks (or tasks you tend to avoid) right before lunch or early in the morning so that you can avoid worrying about them all day.

OVERCOMING PERFECTIONISM

There is no perfect person, and there is no perfect organizational system. Perfectionists can hold themselves and others to high standards, which often leads to better work and better results. However, compulsive perfectionism is oppressive to one's self and others. Striving for perfection causes one to obsess over every detail and causes "analysis paralysis" which rarely produces good results.

Furthermore, a perfectionist can be a terror to work for. Perfectionists tend to micromanage other people's work and can be as ruthlessly unforgiving of others' mistakes as they are of their own mistakes. This dynamic often creates an environment of tension and fear which, besides being unpleasant, is also highly inefficient!

If you are a perfectionist, try to keep in mind the concept of good enough. Don't waste time trying to set up a perfect "work system," or making sure that every product and assignment is 100% perfect before you deem it completed. Ask yourself, *Is it satisfactory?* **Will it do? Will it adequately achieve its intended purpose? Can we move on to the next thing?**

Admittedly, you may be responsible for some tasks and assignments that should be done with meticulous attention to detail, because with these tasks, excellence truly makes a big difference. Just remember that even though any job can be improved, you must manage a finite amount of time and energy, your own and others'.

One manager thinks of it like this: "It's better to just get things done, even if they're not perfect. You have to keep pushing forward. I used to fuss over every little thing, but it's better to be just okay and get it done. The cumulative effect of getting many things done winds up creating much more *excellence* in the end than the intricate finessing of one or two individual things. A whole lot of okay things can add up to a pretty solid foundation. And if you do 'good enough' enough times, it actually gets better, and then suddenly it's *really good!* That's *my* efficiency secret."

■ THE PRINCIPLES FOR GETTING THINGS DONE

- ■ Figure out what time of day you are usually at your best. Attack your most challenging work in your most productive hours. For example, if you feel most energetic between 9 and 11 a.m., use that time to tackle creative tasks. If you get a little drowsy after lunch, perhaps use that time to answer email or phone messages, or to open your mail.

■ When you have trouble remembering certain things, link those things together with other things that you do routinely. For example, if you sometimes forget to return phone calls, do all your phone calling at the same time you pick up your messages. If you find that you often forget to put change in parking meters, tape a quarter to your dashboard.

■ If at any point, you find your work is not up to your own standards, or you haven't met your goals on time, or you've disappointed someone else, *don't waste time blaming yourself.* Just pick up from where you are, and do the best you can. It gets better.

■ Focus on one task at a time.

■ Estimate the time you need to complete a given task, and then add 20% to your estimate.

■ Estimate how much quiet time you need each day or week to do your work, and budget that time.

■ Set up a daily and weekly to-do schedule. Write them in a pocket notebook or on a yellow pad.

■ Periodically look at your habits and routines, and see if you can think of new ways to streamline or combine them.

■ Continually look for new, creative ways to improve efficiency, and ask for suggestions.

Chapter 3

■ Communication And Motivation

*"To effectively communicate, we must realize
that we are all different in the way we perceive
the world and use this understanding as a
guide to our communication with others."*

— ANTHONY ROBBINS

*"Kind words do not cost much.
Yet they accomplish much."*

— BLAISE PASCAL

Clear communication channels and motivated personnel make work run smoothly and contribute to good
time efficiency. When employees understand you and feel
respected by you, you don't have to waste time soothing
wounded egos, negotiating prickly attitudes, or explaining
how you want things done over and over again.

■ BRINGING OUT THE BEST

One of your responsibilities as a manager is to bring out the best in your employees. There are two components to this:

■ **Discern what work or tasks each employee is best suited for or can most naturally grow into.**

■ **Keep employees excited and motivated in their work.**

Discerning the talents of your employees is certainly difficult because people are complicated, and they change and grow in unpredictable ways. Begin by recognizing that any person's ultimate potential (like your own) is a fathomless mystery.

However, there are ways to assess how well an employee is likely to do at a given job. Begin with the evidence at hand: What has this employee done so far? What have they excelled at? What tasks have they performed unsatisfactorily? What seem to be their primary aptitudes?

Next, *listen.* What does this person tell you is important to him or her? When you understand an employee as an individual, when you can imagine the situation from your employee's perspective—including his or her desires, fears, and ambitions regarding the job—then you can confidently move that employee into the most appropriate position.

But you must remain flexible. Be receptive to employees' concerns, as well as nonverbal indications of satisfaction or dissatisfaction with their responsibilities. If someone is obviously assigned the wrong job, transfer them elsewhere.

Most importantly, *be absolutely clear* about your own expectations. When employees know precisely what standards must be met in a given position, then they can thoroughly understand what it takes to really "shine." This knowledge is a potent motivator.

Milt, who advised three different mayors in the area of labor relations, adds, "The leader or administrator has to be motivated himself. He has to be dedicated and he has to have a real emotional involvement in what the bigger picture is. Then he has to communicate that involvement; he has to sell the overall picture to his workers."

■ BRINGING OUT THE BEST

Make a list of the individuals and positions whom you supervise on a regular basis.

_____

_____

_____

_____

Now, for each position, draw up a list of specific measurable performance standards (if you don't already have one) that your employees should meet.

_____

_____

_____

_____

Of those listed, who seem both competent and satisfied in their respective positions?

_____

_____

_____

Who seem either incompetent or unsatisfied in their positions?

_____

_____

Next to the names on the list above, make a note of aptitudes and skills you perceive in these individuals that they are not utilizing in their current positions. Can you think of other roles that these individuals might serve in your organization, for which they may be better suited?

■ MOTIVATION

As a manager, it is important to remember that everyone wants to feel that their work is meaningful. Everyone wants to do a good job.

Shirley Melnicoe, the Executive Director of a social service agency (Northern California Service League) that places ex-offenders in jobs and housing, etc., explains that her staff "needs to know what the big picture is and why we're doing this work, so I talk to them about things like how much incarceration costs the state, and how much we're saving each time we get someone a job or keep them out of prison, and what it means to the community."

Jim Morgan, who owns and manages a commercial print shop says that: "People like to work, particularly if they see a tie-in between their job and what they want to get out of their own lives. Work has to help them achieve their life goals either in a primary way or in a secondary way. A secondary way means that by doing the work, they will get to spend time with their children, or provide for their families. A primary way would be, for example, the case of a man whom we hired as a bindery worker. He had an interest in computers, so we trained him in computers and he loves it; now he's the best we've ever had in that position. He's surpassed the people that trained him. So he's happier and we're in a stronger position too as a result. Matching people with their interests is helping them in a primary way."

One way to spark your employees' enthusiasm is to give them feedback often. Let them know how they're doing and how their efforts affect the big picture of the entire company. Many people flourish when they receive well-directed and well-deserved praise. "I'm very big on giving 'Attaboys!' and 'Way to go's!'," says one manager. "I do it in all sorts of ways. Maybe it's just an email, or I'll go online and find a funny icon to express my feeling, or sometimes I'll buy them a five-dollar coffee card."

Incentives for outstanding performance can also be big motivators. Incentives may include financial bonuses, opportunities for training and professional development, public recognition, or promotion. It's important to keep in mind though that not everyone is motivated by the exact same thing. One manager says: "Different people are motivated by different things. It's useful to understand that. Some people need praise more than they need money. Other people need security. Some people need a lot of room to move and grow, a lot of flexibility and freedom, while others require a lot of structure."

Some individuals have other, very particular needs and desires. For example, in another manager's company: "We have this one guy who's unbelievably efficient. The only price I have to pay for his incredible efficiency is that he likes to blab, so sometimes I have to just indulge that. Sometimes I'll ignore him because I really need to concentrate, but at other times I feel that listening to him is simply a part of my job. It's what feeds him. It makes him feel connected and valued. So I manage him by keeping him happy."

In general, it is good practice to motivate your employees by helping them to get ahead, and to achieve their own professional goals. Give them greater responsibility, as they demonstrate that they can handle it. Challenge them, but do not overwhelm them. Let them know that they are important.

YOUR EXAMPLE

"Leadership is practiced

not so much in words

as in attitude and in actions."

— HAROLD GENEEN

As a supervisor, your own personality, character, and working style set the keynote for the culture of your whole department.

If you demonstrate personal integrity, choose your words thoughtfully, treat people fairly, refrain from denigrating people behind their backs, and—most importantly —always do what you say you will do, then those who work for you will emulate these habits as well.

Shirley declares, "You have to set an example. If you want your staff to be timely, you have to be on time. My staff knows that I tend to get stuff done a day ahead of time, because you have to allow for things to break or go wrong. It could be the photocopier, it could be an emergency, it could be anything, so you never leave anything till the last minute, and I'm always emphasizing that to my staff."

Jim Morgan feels that part of being a leader is also "being aware of what people's interests are and what they want to get out of life, and supporting them in getting where they want to go, unless for some reason it's in conflict with where you want the business to go. But I've never found that to be the case yet."

Barry Newborn, the Director of Sales at a publishing company, also believes in the importance of knowing his staff as individuals. "I once heard a pastor say, 'God realizes the individuality of each one of us. He doesn't even make two snowflakes alike.' A good manager has to be a little bit of a psychologist. Not everyone will do things in exactly the same way, or respond to things in the same way. A lot of people who have the title 'manager' are actually managing tasks instead of people. But if you manage people, and you do it right, the tasks get done," adds Barry.

Shirley agrees. "If you understand what your staff people are going through, they'll respond to you better, because you're not treating them like robots. People do things for people. They may have a job, but how well they do the job will depend a lot on you."

No one is perfect, though. If you are not (yet) a paragon of virtue and equanimity in the workplace, don't feel alone.

Some managers take pride simply in what they don't do. "I think my strongest point is that I don't panic anymore," reflects one manager. "I think it's really useful if the person in charge isn't freaking out."

■ EVALUATE YOURSELF

Take a moment to evaluate your own personal strengths and weaknesses, in terms of the mood you set, and the ways in which you conduct yourself as a manager. What are some positive character traits that you exhibit on a regular basis:

_____

_____

_____

What character traits do you exhibit that could be improved:

_____

_____

_____

RESPECT

R-E-S-P-E-C-T

"Find out what it means to me!"

— Aretha Franklin

There is no quality more important to a healthy working culture than respect.

Respect is a two-way street. If you want your employees and coworkers to respect you, you have to treat them with unflagging respect. It is *especially* important for you to be respectful if you are in a position of power over others. Employees will respond enthusiastically to respectful treatment. According to one employee, "I feel like my boss sees me as valuable, and that helps me see my own value too."

Respect begins with *clear communication.* For example, it is respectful to inform employees well in advance of any changes in policies or procedures. Abrupt surprises are not respectful.

Because you are their supervisor, it is your responsibility to make sure that your employees understand you. Do not get annoyed when a coworker asks for an additional explanation of some task or problem. Take the time to ask, "Is that clear? Do you have any questions? Would you like me to show you? Are you okay?"

Because you are human (and probably under stress), sometimes you'll blow it. You may snap, place blame inappropriately, have an insensitive moment, or simply be mistaken about something. That's all right, but it is absolutely essential that you sincerely apologize. You will not lose any esteem with your coworkers. Your staff understands that you're human, and they'll trust you more if you can admit your mistakes.

"Do I ever apologize? Absolutely," says Barry. "I think, in some instances, *not* apologizing diminishes you as a manager. A lot of times we lose sight of the fact that we're only people, just like the people who report to us. It's okay if they see the good, the bad, and the ugly. I can apologize in a heartbeat. It doesn't make me less of a manager, but it makes me more of a person."

"There are lots of different ways of apologizing," points out Milt. "You can go to a person privately and apologize, you can do it publicly in a group, or you just can do something for that person without saying anything about an apology—it could be a promotion, a pat on the back, an increase in their assignment, or just inviting them to lunch and talking about things. Depending on the situation and the individual involved, there's many ways to apologize, and to communicate respect."

Be diligent about small courtesies and kindnesses, such as knocking before entering a coworker's office (even if the door is open), remembering birthdays (write them on your calendar), asking "How are you?" (and genuinely listening to the answer), and remembering to express concern if a coworker has a close relative in the hospital or is going through a personal crisis such as a divorce.

Understand that this is not about being liked. Though being liked is a fringe benefit of behaving respectfully, it should not be your motivation for doing so. Be respectful because people deserve respect, as do you.

RESPECTFUL CRITICISM

"It's a rare person who wants to hear
what he doesn't want to hear."

— DICK CAVETT

You have an outstanding employee, who has been working for you now almost a year. She does everything well and efficiently, but there is one problem. Every time you ask for something to be done a little differently—at the slightest *hint* of any criticism—she bursts into tears.

Lately, for the last couple of weeks or so, you notice that she's been spending a lot of time on the phone with personal calls. You know that her mother has been ill, but you are not sure if this is why she is on the phone so much. When she's on the phone, she talks loudly and laughs often. It's becoming a distraction for you and possibly for others in the office. Although she still completes her work in a timely fashion, her behavior borders on being professionally inappropriate, in your view. Will you address the phone call issue with her? If so, how will you approach her? What will you say?

Offering constructive criticism is one of the most difficult and delicate obligations of managing. You have to strike a very fine balance; you must be careful and sensitive. It is never easy to criticize, or to receive criticism, but criticism doesn't have to be painful or destructive if we remain respectful and follow some basic principles.

The first principle of constructive criticism is to avoid blaming your employee at the outset. Do not frame the situation in terms of the employee's performance deficit or lack of competence. Begin by pointing out what is going on that isn't working as well as it should. Discuss the process or the product at issue, rather than the employee himself. This can be tricky. If possible, make "I" statements. For example, "I'm feeling some concern lately that this work isn't coming out the way I'd like it to."

Help your employee to do better. Be specific about what you'd like to see done differently, and *how* it could be done differently. (Don't forget to also point out those things that your employee does *right*.) Ask your employee respectfully about his work method, and suggest a different method if you see one that might work better.

Obtain agreement about the situation. Ask your employee for suggestions as to how he thinks the situation can be improved. Perhaps he sees something you don't. Create a detailed job description together with your employee, with measurable performance objectives that your employee can understand and strive for. Sometimes, simply defining a job more distinctly can make everyone happier.

Ask your employee if there is any particular aspect of his job that *he* finds difficult or uncomfortable. Ask, "What can I do to help you?" If your employee is unhappy, consider it your task to make him happy. Ask him what he needs. If an employee is not performing up to par, there may be a reason for this that you could never have guessed, such as a personal issue. Get on your employee's side.

Praise in public; admonish in private. Don't criticize an employee in front of others. ***Never*** make an employee feel worthless, or imply that an employee is a bad person. Occasionally, a worker may insist on being uncooperative or will show no improvement even after you've tried to work with him. In such cases, you must document the problem behavior, or take other necessary action, up to and including dismissal.

But as a general rule, just remember that it is much more important to make employees happy than to tell them that the wastebasket should be on the right side of the desk rather than the left side. The bottom line is that a happy employee is a much more efficient than an unhappy employee.

LETTING EMPLOYEES GO

If you have the authority to hire and fire, it may be your unpleasant duty to take ultimate action, even with someone you like personally.

"You have to make sure your business runs well, not just for yourself but for all the people involved," reflects Jim Morgan. "It's your responsibility, when you realize that somebody does not meet your particular business culture, to let the person go. It's not saying anything bad about the person; it's just not a match. It took me a long time to learn that. The worst case was a lovely woman, a very nice person that we all liked a lot. But I knew on the first day, definitely on the second, that her temperament was wrong for our business. It took me *six years* to let her go. I've gotten a lot better since then. I owe it to the rest of my staff to find people that will be a match. And the people that I've let go — they've all found jobs where they're happier, where they're more of a match!"

Hopefully, there is a "right job" out there for everyone. But you are not ultimately responsible for your employees' lives. Your responsibility is to maintain a work environment that is harmonious and efficient for yourself and your subordinates. If an employee chronically injects dissonance and inefficiency into the workplace, then that employee, sadly, must go.

Chapter 4

■ Good Meetings

"Successful meetings require good planning and a clear agenda. This, in turn, requires strong leadership."
— IRENE DOO, PRESIDENT TEXMATYC

"There is nothing so annoying as to have two people talking when you're busy interrupting."
— MARK TWAIN

Everyone knows what a bad meeting is like: constant interruptions, contentious people, and going over the scheduled time. But what does a good meeting look like? Good meetings use time well. Before you walk into a meeting, you should be completely clear about the specific purpose(s) of the meeting, what you hope to accomplish, and how long you intend to meet.

WHY MEET?

There are many reasons to call a meeting including:

■ **To plan and strategize new projects**

■ **To discuss changes in policy or staffing**

■ **To check in and discuss progress with ongoing projects and tasks**

■ **To fix glitches in teamwork, and resolve conflict**

■ **To exchange information with other managers concerning cooperation and support between departments**

WHO SHOULD COME TO A MEETING?

As a rule, the smaller the meeting, the better. Fewer people can usually "put their heads together" more quickly and productively than a large group can. So, only those who truly need to be at a particular meeting should be invited.

Sometimes, you might invite an additional person to sit in for one reason or another, perhaps to absorb information, or to simply observe your meeting process. Make sure that person's role is clear to everyone present.

■ MEETING AGENDA

Distribute the agenda two or three days in advance so that everyone can come prepared and focused. In the agenda, state the objective(s) and the start and end time for the meeting. Try and make your agenda concise and interesting, and list the most important items first. Include any necessary support documentation with the agenda, but err on the side of omission. It's best not to load meeting participants down with paper; they probably won't read all of it anyway.

Similarly, if others are bringing handouts to the meeting, encourage them to present their data in the form of charts, graphs, or tables. A graphic representation is usually more immediately understandable than a verbal one, and it also makes for a more handy reference tool.

WHEN SHOULD YOU MEET?

If you want to keep your meeting focused and efficient, schedule it for the hour before lunch. It is remarkable how directly people can resolve issues when they're hungry.

By contrast, the hour after lunch is probably the most sluggish, so don't schedule a meeting then if you really want to accomplish anything. If the meeting is simply your weekly staff check-in, then an early afternoon time might be fine.

Avoid Friday meetings; people are already one foot into the weekend, and they're tired from a long week.

Try and keep meeting times down to an hour; you'll lose a lot of people's attention if you don't. Start on time, no matter what—even if the "big boss" hasn't arrived yet. This shows respect to your coworkers who have shown up promptly, and it reinforces the expectation that meetings start as scheduled. You can figure out how to fill in late-comers afterward, or assign someone else to do so.

WHERE TO MEET?

Try and find a pleasant meeting place, with comfortable chairs, a table, good lighting, and minimal distractions. If you meet regularly, arrange a change of scenery once in a while, such as an outdoor setting.

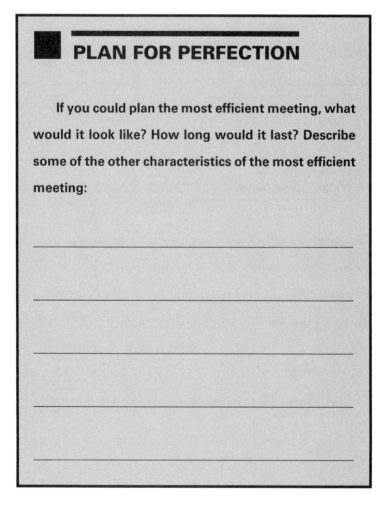

PLAN FOR PERFECTION

If you could plan the most efficient meeting, what would it look like? How long would it last? Describe some of the other characteristics of the most efficient meeting:

_____

_____

_____

_____

_____

FACILITATING THE MEETING

First, welcome everyone. Take a minute or two to say hello, and let people decompress. If relevant, briefly review the last meeting and ask people how they felt about it. Find out what has been accomplished since, and who has followed through on what (and who has not). Review your agenda, and briefly restate what you're there to do. This reinforces the idea that the meeting is a springboard to action, not just a talking session.

As the meeting progresses, stick to your agenda. If you did it right, the first items should be the most important ones. Solicit everyone's input. Ask shy or quiet people direct questions; this is a meeting of the minds and everyone's contribution matters. If you have a quiet contingent that sits together, you might even walk up to them and ask questions.

Spread credit around generously. Express appreciation often for people's accomplishments and ideas. This stimulates involvement and strengthens a climate of respect. Allow people to let off steam and to talk about challenges or difficulty with work. Brainstorm solutions with the group. Do not, however, permit a chronic complainer to dominate discussion.

Remember that a rigid, inflexible atmosphere stifles creative thinking. Keep the discussion on track, but allow a little humor and informality. Encourage people to voice their opinions and suggestions openly and directly. Even if you disagree, acknowledge the value in any sincerely offered point of view.

Brainstorm about best-case scenarios, worst-case scenarios, risks, consequences, and likely outcomes of any given course of action. Decide on a plan of action, integrating as many people's ideas as possible. Obtain group consensus on your chosen plan of action. Make sure everyone leaves the meeting knowing what they personally are responsible for, and by when, in order to carry forward the plan.

After a good meeting, there is a tangible sense of heightened morale. Even if you have to deliver bad news during the meeting, people can leave with a positive attitude if they trust you, and they understand clearly what to expect next.

Once in a while, you might introduce a little variety by asking a coworker to facilitate a meeting. You could even rotate facilitators on a regular basis, depending on your sense of how well your staff can fulfill this responsibility. "My directors are in charge of meetings on a rotation basis," says Shirley. "They set the agenda: they can have trainings, they can have reports, or a combination of both. That way, everybody's buying in to the organization."

 ## SNAGS AND DISTRACTERS

There are any number of factors that can derail a smooth meeting, and you're probably familiar with most of them.

An excess of available snack food and drink can be distracting. Interruptions from outside the room can also occur. You may want to consider posting a sign that says: "Meeting in progress. Do not interrupt except in event of fire or earthquake."

But of course, the primary causes of diversion and distraction at meetings lie in the personalities of meeting participants. Now you might be tempted to think, "If only he were not so stubborn! If only she were not so sensitive! If only he wouldn't be so long winded! If only she would learn to listen! Meetings would be so much easier!" It's better not to think this way. You're simply faced with the human condition. People have their quirks, and it's your job to work with them.

For example, let's say someone makes a comment that is off the subject. If you can, take the heat off the person by assuming responsibility by saying, "I'm afraid I may have said something that got us off topic." Calmly point out that a new subject of conversation has now been introduced, and ask the group if they feel it should be added to the agenda. If not, suggest tabling it for a future meeting. Or, if someone tries to monopolize the conversation, interrupt and say, "Thanks, Donald. I think I see what you're getting at here, but I want to hear from the rest of the group too. Mary, what do you think?"

Some people may use giving a report as an occasion to hold the floor for an inordinate length of time. This can be tricky, because the group may need to hear what they have to say, but if they go on and on, you can induce them to get to the point by asking pointed questions. Don't let them turn their reports into performances.

Side-talking and whispering is another prevalent problem, particularly at larger meetings. One thing you can do, if you're standing, is walk in the direction of the talkers. That usually quiets them quickly. Or you can take a more direct approach: "Excuse me, I can't hear what Stephanie is saying. Janice, Mitch, is there something you want to share with the group? Please everyone, I must insist that you refrain from side conversations. I need everyone's attention and cooperation here. Thanks." You have a right to be annoyed, but it is best to remain polite.

Some people have difficulty articulating their thoughts, and they take a lot of time groping for the right words. Depending on how much of a hurry you're in, give them a minute or so. It's not their fault that their brains won't translate thoughts easily into words; this is a common difficulty. If you need to move along, however, ask, "Do you mean... (inserting a quick paraphrase of what the person seems to be trying to say)?" Chances are, if you were listening (and you have to listen well, *especially* to inarticulate employees), you'll get it right, and the person will feel grateful to be understood.

If a coworker is being obstinate or argumentative, toss it to the group. Ask, "So how do people feel about John's point? Do you agree?" If the answer is a resounding consensual "no!" but John insists on continuing to advocate his opinion, remind John that meeting time is limited and you need to move on. If John still gripes, tell him you'll talk about it privately with him later.

If, on the other hand, John has won converts, and there is a dramatic split on a matter of importance, then you need to delve deeper into the subject, brainstorming possible contingencies, merits, and drawbacks. If the difference of opinion feels acrimonious, it might be best first to reiterate a few points that everyone agrees on.

Keep in mind that, as a rule, people respond well to being recognized for what they do right. So reinforce good habits by giving credit. "I really appreciate how succinctly you made your points in the meeting." Or "I admire how well you listen to people. You are very articulate." This type of praise is probably best given privately, after the meeting is over. Otherwise, in the context of the group, you run the risk of sounding condescending.

 PREPARE FOR DISTRACTERS

Be honest. Who, on your staff, is occasionally (or often) disruptive in meetings?

NAME	BEHAVIOR	PLAN

Next to each person's name, write down what the disruptive behavior is that this person is normally guilty of. For example, interrupting, side talking, not listening, arguing, talking for too long, etc. Now, think of something you can say in one sentence to each person, the next time he or she exhibits this undesirable behavior. Write that sentence down next to the person's name.

When you're actually in a meeting and a staff member is being disruptive, angry and unskillful words may spring to mind in the moment. But formulating your thoughts now about what to say then will help you feel more in control.

RESOLVING CONFLICT

Sometimes, two or more people compete or clash at meetings. If possible, try and defuse the conflict then and there by emphasizing points of agreement and drawing attention to their common objectives, or by quickly bringing other, neutral participants into the discussion.

Unfortunately, sometimes conflicts may be more personal than they appear on the surface, which makes them nearly impossible to settle in a forum such as a group meeting. If you sense that this is what is going on, tell the combatants that you will meet separately with them later, and ask that they allow the discussion to move on for the time being.

When you do meet separately with employees that are in conflict with each other, try and get at the root of the conflict. Allow each person to air their thoughts and feelings. Are they angry with each other over something personal? Do they simply not get along? If so, try to find a way to make it so that they don't need to work together as much. You are not in the business of relationship counseling here; your task is simply to facilitate smooth work operations.

If the conflict is truly based on something pertaining to

the job itself, ask yourself: Do they have radically different ideas about what's best for the department? Are they upset with one another's approaches to a particular task or challenge? If they do simply disagree about approach, be sure to thank them for caring about their work so much. Depending on how severe or irreconcilable the disagreement seems to be, you may still need to find a way of keeping them distant from each other at work. Or you might work with them to find common ground, and a compromise approach that they can both be reasonably happy with.

Often, with conflict, it's hard to tell what's personal and what is not. People sometimes don't even realize why they get so invested in their opinions. Your task, as the peacekeeper and adjudicator, is to remain calm and impartial, and to look for the simplest solution that can satisfy everyone and allow work to proceed.

THE BEST MEETINGS OF ALL

Sometimes, the best meetings are the ones you don't have. Avoiding unnecessary meetings can save you a ton of time. Often times, all you really need to do is talk to a few specific people, or send out a memo to settle what would take twice as long in a meeting.

Some companies utilize log books or bulletin boards for communications that might otherwise require staff meetings. Think about it. Have you been to any meetings in the last year that could just as easily been "held" via email? Have you got any similar meetings currently scheduled?

Chapter 5

■ The Delicate Art Of Delegating

"Don't tell people how to do things,

tell them what to do and let them

surprise you with their results."

— GEORGE S. PATTON

"No person will make a great business

who wants to do it all himself

or get all the credit."

— ANDREW CARNEGIE

You are, even in your role as manager, only one part of a team. In a sense, you're the quarterback—you call the plays. And a skilled quarterback knows when it's time to hand off the ball.

WHY DELEGATE?

"In the beginning (of my career)," recalls Debra, "I wanted to do all the important work myself. I didn't like explaining things to people; it seemed easier to just do it myself. But I've got people working for me now that are skilled and motivated, and they can handle responsibility, which takes a lot of stress off of me."

The purpose of delegating is to free up your time to focus on the specific tasks and projects you are uniquely qualified to perform. Delegation also elevates the morale of your employees, who feel honored by your confidence in their abilities, and can feel proud when they successfully complete the delegated project.

Delegation is not simply asking somebody to do a task. Delegation is investing someone with the *responsibility* to see through a component of the work mission, and granting this person the *authority to make decisions* about how to do it. Being a delegate gives your employee an opportunity to learn and find new meaning in their work.

It can be scary to delegate because it involves relinquishing a degree of control. What if your delegate fails to do as good or as thorough a job as you would have done? Well, that is certainly a possibility but they also may do a fabulous job and become a happier and more productive employee.

In today's business climate, delegation is an absolute necessity, as managers are given more responsibility and less time to complete tasks. By delegating, you are not shirking your responsibility. Quite the contrary, you are *sharing* responsibility, which is precisely what an effective leader does. In any case, you are still going to be accountable for the final outcome. Admittedly, delegation does bring risk. But over time, the risks of not delegating are much greater, to your own health and sanity, and for the productivity, efficiency, and morale of your department.

 ## WHAT SHOULD YOU DELEGATE?

Delegate everything you can. Does this statement sound radical? What can be more important than saving yourself time and energy? Don't be afraid to think "outside of the box" when it comes to delegation!

■ TO DELEGATE OR NOT
TO DELEGATE

Make a list of the tasks and decisions that you are
routinely responsible for:

_____

_____

_____

_____

_____

_____

_____

_____

Now, about each one, ask yourself:

■ Is there anyone else in my department who is qualified to do this, or to make this decision on my behalf?

_____

■ If someone makes a different decision than I would make about this, or performs this task in a different way, would that be likely to cause a significant problem? Or could I live with it?

_____

■ Which of the above jobs and decisions am I sure that I—and no one else—should be the one to do?

_____

Don't be surprised if, after all, relatively few items on your list fall into the last category. Everything else is fair game for delegating.

"I don't delegate long-range and strategic planning," says Jim Morgan. "I do delegate day-to-day operations." "Delegation is about knowing my priorities and objectives," states Barry. "If a task doesn't fall within my job description, I have no problem passing it along to someone else. If someone calls me wanting information about a product, I can let one of my sales reps take care of it. There are also certain types of reports that I can ask someone else to generate for me."

TO WHOM SHOULD YOU DELEGATE?

Never give anyone a job if you're not confident he or she can accomplish it. Assess your prospective delegate's strengths and weaknesses. Is this person creative, flexible, meticulous, experienced, and responsible enough to carry out this duty? Begin by asking yourself what qualities are required for this particular task or what background knowledge is necessary, then match this need with a particular person's skills.

■ PLAN TO DELEGATE

Choose one item from your previous list that you have determined you may be able to delegate in the future. Make a list of the qualities and skills that an appropriate delegate will need.

_____

_____

_____

Now think about your coworkers. Who comes to mind as a plausible delegate?

_____

Remember, you should not delegate to people who are already overloaded with work unless you can authorize them to set aside their current workload, or pass some of it over to another employee. Sometimes, it is both reasonable and necessary to delegate a task to an outside specialist (contractor).

A note of caution: Once you have delegated, it is essential that you do not micromanage your delegates. Give them a chance to do the job without breathing down their necks.

WHAT YOUR DELEGATE NEEDS FROM YOU

Delegates need a clear and detailed understanding of what they are being asked to accomplish. You must articulate a comprehensive vision of what you want to see done, and what you want it to look like. It should go without saying that you yourself should be thoroughly familiar with the work that you are delegating. You must give your delegate all necessary information, as well as access to all necessary resources for completing the assignment.

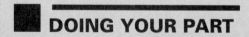

DOING YOUR PART

Consider the task you identified in the last exercise, and imagine that you are in the process of delegating it. List on the following page what your delegate would need to know and what resources you would need to provide.

_____

_____

_____

_____

_____

_____

When you are explaining the task to them, encourage delegates to ask questions and let them know that you will be available to answer further questions throughout the process, and to provide any needed assistance. Emphasize that your delegate should not hesitate to come to you for help.

If your delegates ever *look* nervous, ask what's wrong. It's natural to feel anxious about a new responsibility. Don't just say, "Nonsense! You'll be fine!" Discuss specifically what they are afraid might happen. Which elements of the delegated project seem worrisome at the outset? Maybe you can help with those when they come up, or maybe someone else can. Or perhaps you can explain why these challenges won't really be so difficult.

It is very important to agree on deadlines. Make sure delegates understand the scope of the work they are assuming, and come to an agreement with them on an explicit timeline, including checkpoints if necessary. Finally, make it clear to your delegates that you trust them and that you are relying on them to make choices and to use their imagination and judgment.

 ## MOTIVATING YOUR DELEGATE

If you exude confidence in your delegates, they will be more likely to live up to—or even exceed—your expectations. One way to express confidence is to invoke their past successes and accomplishments. For example, say, "I know you can do this because you're so excellent at _____. Really, this project isn't much different. It just involves one or two other things." Or: "You know, a few months ago you really impressed everyone with your work on _____. I've seen your work; I know that given a chance, you can knock our socks off."

If your delegate will be working with other people on the given project, take the person around, introduce the person (if necessary), explain to everyone the important role that your delegate will play in completing the project, and publicly express your positive feelings about your delegate at every opportunity.

Pitch in and help when necessary. Show your delegate the best way to do things, if they appear to be floundering. Don't blame. Remember, it was your choice to entrust this person with these responsibilities. Most important of all, once the work is accomplished, take the time to be thorough and generous with your praise.

■ THE RESPONSIBILITY IS STILL YOURS

Yes it's true. The bad news about delegating is that it all comes down to you anyway—your judgment, and your responsibility for the final product.

It may be wise to have your delegates report to you on a regular basis, or even to keep a log of their work, so that you can check it when you want to. You might even create a project status form that lists the specific steps of the project so that you can track a project's status.

"When you give someone responsibilities, you have to follow up," notes Milt. "You have to know on any given day where a person is at in relationship to her responsibilities. Sometimes, you might find that your expectations have been completely off base, so you have to change them."

The good news is that even if your delegate does not perform up to your expectations, there are hidden benefits of delegating. These include:

- What you may learn about your delegate's abilities

- What you may learn about alternate ways of accomplishing tasks that you've always done before in a particular way

- An enhanced sense of ownership, or "buy-in" of your department's mission among coworkers

- Perhaps most significantly, time to develop or attend to other important projects that you have been keeping on the back burner, such as long-range planning and periodic reviews of forms and processes

All in all, sooner or later, you must delegate, or you will burn yourself out. And it's better for you, your company, and your employees for you not to learn this the hard way.

Chapter 6

■ Handling Problems Efficiently

"We can't solve problems by using the same kind of thinking we used when we created them."
— ALBERT EINSTEIN

"Expect problems and eat them for breakfast."
— ALFRED MONTAPERT

Problems are time-consuming. Solving problems efficiently will help fulfill the mission of your organization and streamline your time.

COMMON TYPES OF PROBLEMS

All kinds of problems can arise at work, some more predictable and fixable than others. Here's a list of some common types of problems you might face or encounter:

- **Missing materials**
- **Miscommunication**
- **Conflict**
- **Lack of adequate time to complete projects or tasks**
- **Lack of adequate and timely information**
- **Inadequate or unpleasant working conditions**
- **Flawed or inefficient procedures**
- **Bottleneck in the process**
- **Unsatisfying work**
- **Inept employee**
- **Poor teamwork; lack of adequate communication**
- **High turnover**
- **Low morale**
- **Mistakes**
- **Safety hazards**

You can not begin solving a problem until you have defined it.

■ DEFINING PROBLEMS

One thing to keep in mind when you're trying to define a problem is that few work-related problems are attributable, at their root, to individual employees or outside forces. The vast majority of work-related problems are caused by flaws in the system—including the way things are done and the way procedures are set up. This doesn't mean it's *your* fault; it just means that the first place you should look is at the system itself, not at individuals, especially if it's a recurring problem.

Sometimes the issue at hand is merely a symptom of a larger problem. Begin to gather information but gather it carefully. You may need to review documents such as records and reports, and you may need to talk with several different people about the situation. Their opinions will be based on their own points of view, biases, and self-interest, and you will have to sort through all this to get to the heart of the matter.

Be bold. You may have to design a whole new way of doing things in order to solve the problem.

ANALYZING PROBLEMS

Imagine a particular problem you are facing at work. Write down the problem, including every element, every possible cause, every pertinent factor. Then answer these basic questions:

What are the undesirable outcomes caused by this problem?

_____

_____

What conditions influence this situation?

_____

_____

Do I have to solve this problem myself, or can I enlist help?

_____

Who can help me with this problem?

_____

Do I have the authority to make final decisions in regard to this problem?

_____

Do I have enough information to tackle this problem?

_____

Where can I get the information I need to address this problem?

_____

Whom can I turn to for useful insights or information regarding this problem?

_____

What benefits will proceed from solving the problem?

_____

Just how important are these benefits?

_____

If the problem involves an isolated task that is performed as part of a particular process, you might also ask:

- ■ **Is this a new task?**

- ■ **Why is this operation performed?**

- ■ **Are there any unnecessary steps in this operation?**

- ■ **Could this task be combined with another?**

- ■ **Could this task be eliminated?**

- ■ **Should the sequence of steps involved in this task be altered or simplified?**

- ■ **Is the person (people) assigned to this task qualified to do it?**

- ■ **Is this task challenging enough for the person (people) doing it?**

In a complex situation, when you're dealing with multiple influencing factors and points of view, wait until you've done all your data gathering before you make a judgment.

Try not to develop a theory prematurely ("Employee X is the problem!"), because that might lead you to disregard later evidence that would contradict or compromise your theory.

Of course you have to set some limits on your investigation, based on your available time, the scope, and the impact of the problem.

Once you have all your data in front of you, decide which data is most reliable and significant. You might also order your data in terms of cause and effect, or chronology of events.

 ## ATTITUDE FOR ADDRESSING PROBLEMS

REMAIN CALM AND RESPECTFUL. You need your staff's loyalty and trust as much as you need good information. If you vent frustration or show temper, you're likely to discourage co-operation, and co-workers might fear to be open with you.

LISTEN CAREFULLY. Let other people do lots of talking. Encourage creative input and suggestions for solving the problem.

IF YOU GET OVERWHELMED, RELAX. Turn your attention away from the problem for a while. Let your subconscious mind do a little work on it without your help.

As you start to engage with possible solutions to your problem, here are the types of questions you should be answering:

- **Can we eliminate or combine anything?**

- **Do we need to improve or create a new product or service?**

■ CHOOSING SOLUTIONS

For a complex problem, explore multiple alternative solutions. Ask yourself:

- **Which solution is most likely to produce tangible results most quickly?**

- **Which of these solutions have been applied before, and what have been the results?**

■ **What difficulties are involved with each solution?**

■ **Which of these solutions will my superiors in the company most likely approve of? Which might they object to, and why?**

Look at the best elements of each possible solution and consider combining elements of different solutions. Recruit staff to help implement your chosen solution. Assign clear and specific responsibilities. Get outside help too if necessary. Set up a timetable for implementing your solution. Include checkpoints and measurable progress objectives.

■ GETTING INPUT FROM STAFF

Your staff's experience, as well as your own, is a valuable resource. Everybody involved in a given situation probably has an idea about how to solve the problem, and at least some of these ideas may prove useful.

But whether you follow their suggestions or not, consult your staff. If you do, they will feel respected, and they will be more likely to buy in to the solution you implement.

IMPLEMENTING SOLUTIONS

In implementing solutions, make sure that company policy and union contracts are strictly adhered to, and that the solution you implement is thoroughly consistent with your company's mission. Make sure you have approval from both your own staff, and those above you in your organization. If your chosen solution entails new challenges or responsibilities for your staff, make sure to provide appropriate training and orientation.

Change always involves an element of stress and uncertainty, but change also brings new energy and vitality to a workplace. Once employees have mastered a new system, and they see for themselves that it works better than the old one, their morale and sense of belonging will be strengthened.

A WORD ABOUT CRISES

Most problems are not crises. A crisis is a problem that threatens enormous consequences, and must be addressed immediately. When a crisis does occur, first determine if a similar crisis has occurred in the past, and if so, how it was solved. You may need a different solution this time, but you can still get a useful idea about what to do from what's been done before.

Many of the techniques suggested for addressing non-critical problems can be applied to a crisis as well, except that in a crisis you usually have less time to act and react. Therefore, it is especially important during a crisis to remain calm and flexible, and to share responsibility if you can.

Once the crisis is over, make sure you devise a stream-lined procedure for meeting similar crises in the future, or for preventing this type of crisis from arising again.

EVALUATING YOUR SOLUTION

After a crisis is over, evaluate the success of your chosen solution(s) on the basis of both tangible and intangible criteria, including:

Was it effective?

Was it worth the cost?

_____

Could it have been more efficient?

_____

Describe its long-term applicability.

_____

What effect did it have on staff morale?

_____

What effect did it have on other aspects of work?

_____

Did it addresses the underlying causes of the problem or just its symptoms?

_____

Was it consistent with our mission?

_____

After the solution has been in place for some length of time, you may want to meet with your staff to share perceptions of how well the solution has worked, or is working. If your solution involved a new method of doing something, compare it to the old one, and see if everyone agrees that the new method is better. If possible, prepare charts or tables to graphically illustrate the measurable results of the change.

But what if your solution *didn't* work? The good news is that you now have some new data to work with. You've done a trial run of one solution that didn't work. This may lead to new insights that will help you and your staff more accurately identify the true causes of the problem as well as better solutions. Furthermore, when you openly acknowledge that your proposed changes didn't achieve their desired effect, your subordinates will perceive you as a strong, trustworthy leader.

■ PREVENTING PROBLEMS

Of course, the most efficient solution is to prevent a problem from arising in the first place. Strategies for preventing problems include planning for unexpected absences and for fluctuating workloads, training "understudies" to do important tasks, and periodic department performance evaluations that entail a rapid response to any newly identified glitches or potential problems.

CONTINUAL IMPROVEMENT

Always be on the lookout for ways to save time or labor, enhance safety, increase efficiency, reduce waste, and improve your product. Periodically, if you have the authority to do so, reevaluate the effectiveness of your mission statement. Does it need to change? Does it still accurately describe your organization or department?

Chapter 7

■ Time Wasters, Interruptions, And Distractions

"Never confuse motion with action."

—Benjamin Franklin

■ STAYING ON TRACK

You will get thrown off track occasionally. Don't blame yourself. The important thing is to get back on. But it also helps to be aware of what gets you off track in the first place.

> **The following is a list of common time wasters. Check all those you're guilty of, or that you have to contend with.**

_____ procrastination

_____ ambiguous deadlines

_____ unrealistic deadlines

_____ unclear objectives

_____ trying to do too many things at once
(excessive multitasking)

_____ losing important notes scribbled on scraps
of paper

_____ a cluttered desk

_____ being bogged down in petty details

_____ social interruptions

_____ conversations that go on too long

_____ too many personal phone calls

_____ being unable to say "no"

_____ too many shifting priorities

_____ workplace too small or generally uncomfortable

_____ _____

_____ _____

How much time do you estimate that these time
wasters cumulatively cost you, in a given week?

_____

THAT MONSTER, THE PHONE

Does your telephone run your life? Does a sense of urgency fill your mind whenever it rings? Here is a little secret: You don't have to answer it. "I don't usually answer the phone," says Jim. "There are three or four other people in the office who answer the phone. Then they come and tell me who is on the phone, and I decide whether or not to take the call."

It is not sly or disrespectful to screen your calls. If the call is important, your caller will no doubt leave a message and then after reviewing the message, you can decide how important it is. If it's not important at all, your caller might hang up. Congratulations! You just saved time by avoiding an unnecessary call.

It is perfectly okay to call people back at your convenience. The vast majority of calls do not require urgent attention. In our age of answering machines, voice mail, and email, to pick up the phone each time it rings no matter what else you're in the middle of is exactly like inviting anyone, anytime, to amble into your office and strike up a conversation with you.

Email is a wonderful invention. Make strategic use of email. If someone leaves a simple question on your voice mail, shoot back an email response instead of returning the call. When you're setting up a meeting, don't call everyone! Send out a group email! The reason email is more time-efficient than the telephone is that emails can be brisk and to-the-point, whereas social convention dictates that any phone conversation, however singular its purpose, must include certain pleasantries and courtesies (and more than that if either party really likes to talk).

 MATCHING THE MODE TO THE TASK

Consider the following list of tasks and activities. Which of them normally require phone calls, and which might be accomplished just as well or better via email? Write in "p" for phone or "e" for email next to each one, or "p/e" if it depends on the particular situation.

_____ reviewing a report with someone

_____ setting up an appointment, or lunch date

_____ requesting a copy of a document or record

_____ reporting on the status of a project

_____ offering specific advice to an employee

_____ explaining a procedure

_____ responding to a customer complaint

_____ organizing a special staff meeting

_____ _____

_____ _____

Of course, you can't avoid your phone forever. But try to limit your phone talk time as much as possible. Set specific times of day for people to call you, and to return calls.

When you take a call, try to focus on the conversation right away. If you find yourself in a long phone chat, ask yourself silently, "Is this really important? Is this a major client? Do I really need to be having this conversation right now?" If the answer is that you actually want to get off the phone, try one of the following exit lines:

"You know what? I have to go."

"I'm sorry, I have to go. I'm under a tight deadline."

"Let's finish this conversation in person some time, okay? I should go."

"Listen, it's been nice talking with you, but I really need to get back to what I was doing before you called."

Do whatever works to get off the phone. The other person wants to talk but you don't. Find a way to say "no" to the conversation.

■ THE MAGIC WORD: NO

Many of us are conditioned to be "yes" people. We want to be nice, we don't want to hurt anyone's feelings, we don't want to seem selfish, and we want to be seen as accommodating. Oh but the time that is lost for the lack of a simple word. So easy and yet so difficult to pronounce, why is it so hard to say no?

Understand that when you say "no", you are not saying "no" to the whole person. You are not negating the person's entire being and you are not devaluing the person or dismissing the person's legitimate needs or desires. You are simply saying "yes" to your own needs, your own limits, you own agenda, your own priorities.

Get in the habit of saying "no" and making it stick. Give a reason if you feel you have to. Say, "I'm sorry but I can't. I've just got way too much on my own plate right now." "Sorry, but I have a meeting tonight I need to prepare for."

Nothing will throw you off track more often than reflexively saying "yes" to every request. But don't be discouraged if saying "no" takes a little practice. You've probably been saying "yes" reflexively for a long time, and it takes a while to retrain yourself.

■ SOCIAL INTERRUPTIONS AND LONG TALKERS

You may have noticed that certain people seem to need an audience wherever they go. They'll use the flimsiest excuses to draw you into conversation and regale you with stories. Don't blame these people. Who knows why they need audiences? It is not your job to psychoanalyze them (unless you're a psychotherapist). Your job is to stick to your agenda.

Try this. If someone is needlessly prolonging a conversation (and you need the conversation to conclude), paraphrase what the person has said, like this: "I hear you saying _____. I understand, but we should really have this conversation another time because I need to get back to work right now." Or, try an end of conversation cue phrase like, "Well, the last thing I want to say is..." "Well, before we finish, I'd just like to say..." or, "Okay, I'll start on this right away."

Nonverbal cues can also be effective. If you're standing in the hall, take a half step away from the speaker and glance toward your destination, or if you're in your office, break eye contact and clear your throat quietly. Pick up a pen or a calculator, or reach toward the phone, looking a little distracted. These gestures may work to break the spell.

Shirley observes, "There's a lot in your body language that can tell people to get to the point—or not. If I lean back and just look at them, that says I have time to listen. But if I'm hunched forward over my computer or over something on my desk that I'm in the midst of writing or reading, that sends a different message. If I invite someone to sit down, they'll be here longer. But if, in conversation, I give short answers like, 'Mmm. Okay,' then they can tell I'm busy."

Barry suggests that "You can be very direct without being offensive. When someone asks, 'Do you have a minute?' you can answer, 'Just a minute.' If someone wants to pass on a little business and a little personal information, sometimes I just have to say that I'll take the business information but the personal will have to wait. I can be nice but forceful about that."

Think about it. What else could you possibly say, or do, to signal the end of a conversation? Try to keep your ideas honest and pleasant.

■ A MANAGER IS NOT A COUNSELOR

Some people may come to you with problems all the time, because you're the manager. When this happens, don't automatically put your own work aside to deal with people's difficulties, unless you're truly the one who should be responsible for handling them. If you are not directly responsible, suggest that they ask their coworkers for assistance, or you could refer them to someone else or to useful reference materials. If you find you're always "bailing out" the same person, chances are this person needs to learn to face his own challenges.

"If someone says it's an emergency, you have an obligation to let yourself be interrupted," acknowledges Milt. "However, you should let that person know, if it's a frivolous interruption, that they should be a little more sensitive to your time just as you want to be sensitive to theirs. It's a two-way street."

MORE TIPS FOR REDUCING INTERRUPTIONS

"Rearrange the furniture in your office so that you are facing *away* from the door, or at least so that you can avoid eye contact with passersby; or just close the door!" Barry states, "I try to have an open door policy with all the people that report to me, but there's times when you just have to say "No." When that occurs, my door's closed, there's a note on the door, and somebody has to basically be bleeding for me to let them in. The only people who have access to me at those times are my direct boss and my family."

Make a secret arrangement with a secretary or coworker such that, if someone is visiting in your office for too long, your co-conspirator will interrupt you with something "urgent" so that you can tell your visitor, "Excuse me, we'll have to talk later."

Let people know what the best times are to come and talk to you, with the implicit message that other times are not so good.

Jim offers this idea: "Sometimes I just get out of the office. I think that probably most managers do at some point or another. Sometimes, to get the work done, you need to get away. We have a library just up the street that has cubicles. That sometimes can work. People sometimes work out of their own homes or go to a coffee shop." The thing that's being weighed here is how is your time best used? And what is that you are trying to accomplish?

There is no question about it: Interruptions and distractions by coworkers can wreck your focus and ability to get things done. But remember, if you're like most people, you probably interrupt and distract yourself far more than your coworkers do. When you have a tough project on your desk, how often do you find yourself stepping out of your office to go to the drinking fountain? Or heading to the restroom? Or having a snack? Or checking and rechecking your email? Or surfing the internet? Or engaging in frivolous conversation? The limitation of all of the techniques is that they are limited in coping with a tough project.

THE PROCRASTINATION MONKEY

We all do it. We all put off doing what we have to do when it might be unpleasant or challenging to do. And the longer we put it off, the more creative we are about finding ways to dawdle and procrastinate—the heavier the monkey grows on our backs.

Procrastination is no fun. Think about it: have you ever actually *enjoyed* yourself while you were procrastinating? Of course not. Even if you procrastinate by engaging in some activity that would otherwise be delightful, you can't enjoy it even one-tenth as much as you would *after* you've faced the music and delved into your task.

If procrastination is painful, then why do we do it? The main reason we procrastinate is because we're afraid that we just can't do the thing we have to do, or we are afraid that we won't do it well. This is nonsense. How often have we had this feeling and then proved ourselves wrong? In any event, no task is more daunting or agonizing while you're actually doing it than it is while you're avoiding it. How often have you procrastinated and procrastinated, and then, once you finally started the job, realized, "hey, this isn't so bad"?

There are also a multitude of other reasons why we may procrastinate. Some of us simply have too much going on, too many agenda items which make it difficult for us to focus on a major task. Some people may actually be afraid of success. Some of us are afraid that people may expect more of us (or we may expect more of ourselves) if we accomplish a big job. Or perhaps, we're afraid that once we accomplish the big task, there will be little or nothing left for us to do. Sometimes we simply fear the unknown—the monkey isn't exactly comfortable, but at least he's familiar.

For many of us, our personal procrastination patterns are recurring and habitual. For example, when you have a report to write, do you feel an overwhelming urge to compose a shopping list instead? Or do you suddenly become fascinated by the groupings of people you can see from your window, or by different ways of combing your hair in the mirror, or by the solitaire game on your computer? "So many things can steal you away from your intended project," observes Barry. "Things will happen like, suddenly I notice the blinds aren't straight, so I need to get up and close them."

■ RECOGNIZE YOUR PATTERNS

What are some of your own procrastination routines? What activities (such as eating) or objects (such as the phone) do you often employ for procrastination purposes?

_____

■ OUTWITTING THE MONKEY

Here is a sampling of tried-and-true techniques for getting the procrastination monkey off your back. Try one, try
a few, or combine several. Keep trying until you find a recipe that works for you.

- ■ Break your work down into tiny steps. Ask yourself,
  "What can I do in five minutes that will move this project along? What's my next fifteen-second task?"

■ Do fifteen to twenty minutes of vigorous physical exercise, such as brisk walking, before you start your work. This can settle your mind and clear out your resistance to the task at hand.

■ Set up a formal appointment with yourself to begin working on your task or project. Honor this appointment just as you would honor an appointment with a major client, or your boss, or the President of the United States.

■ If a wave of preoccupations and competing obligations rushes to your mind, make a list of them, and then set the list aside. That way you know they won't disappear and you won't forget them; you can deal with them after your work is finished.

■ Establish a ritual warm-up routine before doing big chunks of challenging work. For example, meditate for ten minutes, clear your desk, say a prayer, and turn off your phone's ringer.

■ Make a list of everything you're afraid can go wrong with your project, and then next to each listed item, write down how you can prevent these problems.

■ Get rid of distractions. Turn your ringer off, hang a "Do Not Disturb" sign on your door, place books and magazines out of your sight, hide your desk radio, disable your modem, close the shade, etc.

■ Start with the easiest, most bearable aspect of the job.

■ Think of the benefits you will reap by completing your task. Consider the consequences of further delay. Connect your task to the "big picture" of your goals.

■ Commit yourself to completing your task (or some clearly defined portion of it) before you get up from your chair again.

■ When you're truly bogged down and tired, let your work project go for a while. Go away for a designated amount of time and refresh yourself. Schedule regular breaks.

■ Try reverse psychology on yourself. See how long you can go doing nothing at all. When you get tired of that, start your work.

■ Set up rewards for finishing your work. Think how much you'll savor those rewards, once you've climbed your mountain of work.

■ Make a game of finding new and creative ways to end procrastination.

No doubt you can imagine other, more unique and un-orthodox methods of overcoming your own procrastina-tion. Try it now. How might you outsmart the monkey the next time he tries to jump on your back?

Chapter 8

■ Unstressing

"A man who suffers or stresses before it is necessary,

suffers more than is necessary."

— SENECA

"Worry and stress affects the circulation, the heart,

the glands, the whole nervous system,

and profoundly affects heart action."

— CHARLES MAYO

Stress is familiar to all of us. The feeling of anxiety, tension, and pressure, experienced in the emotions, mind, and body is a part of life and work; we each have to learn to deal with it. Unless dealt with properly, stress has many deleterious effects. Physically, stress causes muscles to tense up, heart rate to speed up, skin to perspire, and blood pressure to rise. Stress can lead to headaches, lack of sleep, indigestion, and illness. Emotionally, stress gives rise to irritation, anger, anxiety, depression, confusion, fear, and worry. Stress makes concentration difficult and interferes with memory.

Stress can also hurt personal relationships. People who are stressed are often intolerant and impatient, which can make them lash out at the people they're closest to.

Last, but perhaps not least, stress is a big time waster because it leads to bad judgment and inefficient behavior.

■ MOST COMMON CAUSES OF STRESS

If you're feeling stressed and irritable, look at the following list of possible factors and note which ones apply to you.

- ■ **lack of proper rest**

- ■ **lack of control over an unpleasant situation**

- ■ **change in working conditions**

- ■ **trying to do too much at once**

- ■ **lack of leisure time**

- ■ **pent-up emotions such as loneliness, grief, or anger**

■ overuse of coffee or soft drinks

■ improper diet

■ improper lighting

■ relationship trouble

■ tension between coworkers

■ rude customers

■ deadlines

■ financial concerns

■ lack of job security

■ a difficult job

■ the wrong job

Identify which one of the common causes of stress is causing you the most grief. Brainstorm three ways you can change the situation starting tomorrow.

■ RELIEVING STRESS

Sadly, the workplace is a fertile breeding ground for stress. Fortunately, there are many ways to relieve and discharge stress from our system. Here is a sampling of tried-and-true techniques for relieving stress. Try one, try a few, or combine several. Keep trying until you find a recipe that works for you.

■ TALK ABOUT IT Share the burden with someone. Let someone give you the benefit of their wisdom and compassion.

■ EXERCISE Walk, run, swim, play tennis, work out in the gym, or work in the garden. Stress and tension get stored in the body, and can be released with physical exercise. At work, take the opportunity to get up and walk around when you can.

■ DO SOMETHING KIND FOR SOMEONE ELSE This can have two effects. First, it gets your mind off your own troubles. Second, it creates a pleasant feeling between yourself and the other person, and this pleasant feeling will linger with you a while and calm your stress.

■**TAKE THINGS ONE AT A TIME** Don't try to do too much all at once. When work or life seems overwhelming, take a step back. Easy does it.

■**HAVE REASONABLE EXPECTATIONS OF YOUR-SELF** Let yourself off the hook if you find you can't meet the standard of perfection.

■ **ACCEPT WHAT YOU CANNOT CHANGE** At work, and in life, there will be undesirable elements that you can't control, so you might as well not waste time regretting or agonizing over them. Instead, direct your energies to the things you can influence.

■ **SET LIMITS** Set limits on how much energy you'll expend in any one activity. You are not blessed with an inexhaustible energy supply. Know your limits and respect them.

■ **MAKE A LIST OF WHAT'S WEIGHING ON YOU** Once you have it all in front of you on paper, it may not seem so overwhelming.

■ **SET ASIDE TIME FOR LEISURE, RECREATION, FAMILY TIME, OR OTHER ACTIVITIES THAT YOU EN-JOY** Be serious about scheduling this time. Enjoyment is necessary for your overall health and well-being. It will even help you to be a better manager. You must get your mind completely off of work on a regular basis.

■ **MEDITATE** Meditation has been proven to refresh the mind. Sit somewhere quiet and comfortable. Try and sit up as straight as possible, without straining. Close your eyes and just listen to the flow of your breath. Let your thoughts go where they will. Do this for at least ten minutes a day.

■ **ESCAPE SOMEWHERE** Go to the movies, the beach, anywhere you can take a little vacation. Take yourself completely away from the stressful parts of your life, at least for a while. Lose yourself in something relaxing.

■ **SPEND SOME ALONE TIME** Schedule at least a couple of hours a week just to be by yourself. Walk, read, write in your journal, or see a movie. Just take a break from talking and interacting with people. Give yourself to yourself for a little while.

■ **SLEEP MORE** No kidding—not getting enough sleep is a major cause of stress. If you never get quite enough sleep, you forget what it's like to be rested and refreshed. When you are not well rested, problems can get blown out of proportion, and your stress increases. Go to bed earlier, or even take a nap during the day if you can. Even very short naps can have a wonderfully rejuvenating effect on the nervous system.

■ **READ FOR PLEASURE** Get absorbed in an interesting book or magazine. This is an intelligent, non-stressful way to stimulate your mind.

■ **CLEAN THE HOUSE** A clean environment calms and pleases the mind.

■ **TAKE A NICE WARM BATH** Oh yes.

■ **SPEND TIME IN NATURE** Go to a park, a lake, a beach, the woods, or the hills. Breathe the fresh air and walk around. This has a restorative effect on the mind and spirit.

■ **EAT A NUTRITIOUS DIET** Eat more whole grains, fresh vegetables, and fresh fruit. Eat fewer fried foods, less refined sugar, and less red meat. Drink less coffee! A healthier, more nourished body makes for a happier, more contented mind and spirit. A healthier diet may also improve the quality of your sleep.

■ **PLAY OR LISTEN TO MUSIC** Music is magic. Allow yourself to become lost in music once in a while.

■ **HAVE A SENSE OF HUMOR** Learn to laugh at yourself. Take your troubles a little less seriously.

■ **COUNT YOUR BLESSINGS** Every day, think about all the good things in your life, and be grateful for them. Once in a while, make a list of them on paper.

■ **ANSWER NEGATIVE THOUGHTS WITH POSI-TIVE ONES** Give yourself positive messages. If you catch yourself having a discouraging thought, answer it with an encouraging thought. Never allow yourself to put yourself down!

■ **REWARD YOURSELF FOR DOING WELL** Give yourself some kind of treat, such as a family outing, a vacation weekend, or a purchase of something you've long wanted. Pat yourself on the back for a job well done, even if you only do it silently.

■ **PLAN AHEAD FOR CHANGES IN YOUR LIFE AND IN YOUR SCHEDULE** Everything goes smoother and easier with a little foresight and preparation.

■ **AVOID COMMUTE HOUR TRAFFIC** Get up an hour early if you have to. Sitting in rush hour takes its toll on the nerves.

■ **BREATHE DEEPLY** Take a slow, deep, easy breath
or three whenever you think of it.

■ **SPEND QUALITY TIME WITH YOUR LOVED
ONES** Nothing soothes the soul more than the company
of people who care about you and make you happy.

■ STRESS REDUCTION EXERCISES

The following physical motions and exercises can relieve stress stored in the body. You can do them at any
time, right at your desk. For many people, mid-afternoon
seems a natural time for a few stress-release movements.
Remember that releasing stress in the body also clears
your mind, which sharpens your judgment and ultimately
results in better all-around time management.

■ Clench your fist for five seconds. Then let it go and
stretch out your fingers. Do the same with your
other fist.

■ Roll your head around back and forth, slowly, releasing the tension in your neck.

- Try and touch your chin to your chest, to release pressure in the back of your neck.

- Practice tensing up different muscles all along your body from toe to head, and then releasing.

- Release the tension in your forehead by raising your eyebrows up, and then stretching them down.

- Push your shoulders back and breathe deeply, releasing tension from your chest.

- Move your shoulders around, up, and down. Shrug them high and low.

- Massage your forehead, your ears, your cheekbones, and your neck. Apply as much pressure as it takes to squeeze out the tension. Then stretch out your fingers and shake out your hands.

- Take a deep breath of fresh air. Hold it for a moment, and then let it out. Do this three or four times in a row.

STRESS, SELF-MANAGEMENT, AND LIMITS

Sometimes the pressures people feel on the job come largely from their own imaginations. If you feel like you're working under pressure, question how much of the pressure is really there, outside of you. Perhaps the main person who is demanding too much of you is yourself. Ask yourself, "What is it that I am afraid of right now, on this job? What is the worst thing that can possibly happen here, if my fears come true?"

"It's good to know your limitations," notes Barry. "In the process of managing myself, if I am asked to put something else on my plate, and I know that I can't get it done, I can say, 'Hey, right now, I'm sorry. Right now this is more than I have time for.' There's nothing wrong with that. If you miss a deadline, or don't get it done, that'll make you look worse than if you just say, 'Hey look, I can't do it right now.' It's good to be honest about things and not bite off more than you can chew."

"Sometimes I tend to be more critical of myself than I need to be. Taking time to do some internal reflection is really good. When I'm starting to feel not so good about myself, it shows. My wife, who knows me really well, brings it to my attention. She says, 'Barry, you need to loosen your tie.' I've started using that line with myself when I'm alone too."

"You can reduce stress by adhering to the principles of time management: setting your goals and setting your priorities," observes Milt. "But in setting your priorities, you must realize that there are times you have to drop some things in order to maintain your emotional and physical health. That means taking time off and vacations."

CREATIVITY AND ANXIETY

At work, you'll have time that is devoted to routine tasks that you do on a regular basis which require little forethought or imagination and other time that is creative including new projects, report or proposal writing, and interactions of all kinds. It is usually the creative tasks that we find most difficult to organize, because they contain an element of the unpredictable and the unknown.

THE WISDOM TO KNOW
THE DIFFERENCE

We are "hardwired" to feel anxiety about the unknown. List the types of work situations in the coming week that are likely to present you with unknowns, or to which you will need to respond creatively.

_____

_____

_____

_____

_____

Consider your list above. Which of these situations cause you to feel anxious. Is your anxiety about performing well? Or are you anxious about getting things done quickly enough?

You can not entirely eliminate unknowns, at work or anywhere. But one component of time efficiency is the ability to make clear distinctions between what you can control and reasonably predict, and what you can't.

■ SELF CHECK-IN

When you are starting to feel stressed or burned out, consider these questions:

- **Should I and can I take time out?**
- **Am I no longer enjoying my lifestyle?**
- **Why am I restless?**
- **What's bothering me?**
- **Have I got a clear sense of purpose in life?**

Be honest with yourself and look carefully for the answers to these questions. They will tell you a good deal about what you need to do. You may discover that you have to make some courageous changes in your life and/or work situation, or you may need to communicate something difficult to someone, or there may be some other important process or project you have been neglecting. Trust your inner wisdom, and remember that you owe it to yourself and your loved ones to take good care of yourself.

Conclusion Part 1

■ In Your Own Time

"Today is yesterday's plans put into action."

— UNKNOWN

As was stated earlier, time is our most precious currency. Literally, the way we manage our time—at work, at home, or anywhere, is the way we manage our lives.

Managing yourself is as much a function of self-knowledge and self-awareness as it is a function of self-discipline. It is important to regularly evaluate your habits and your actions, and to examine whether they effectively promote your own and others' success and happiness.

■ SELF-EVALUATION

Barry notes that, "There are lots of tools to manage your time, like palm pilots and so forth, but unless you're disciplined enough to *manage yourself,* all those gadgets really won't do you a lot of good."

For a week or so, make a log of all your activities. Then take a few minutes to evaluate your time efficiency. Ask yourself:

- **What do I do particularly well?**

- **What do I tend to avoid?**

- **Which of my actions have generated the best results?**

- **Which of my actions have generated the most disappointing results?**

- **Whom do my actions affect most, on the job?**

- **How do my actions affect these individuals?**

- **Do I waste anyone's time?**

- **Do I respect everyone's time?**

- **Is there anything I do that could be done more efficiently, or even eliminated?**

- **What will I change, once my analysis is completed? Or, would I change anything?**

Be as honest with yourself as you can, and where you're not sure, ask others for feedback. In fact, the more you're responsible for, the more essential it is for you to get periodic feedback from staff.

It may be wise to establish a relationship with a co-worker (whose judgment you respect) in which you regularly evaluate each other, formally or informally.

Finally, evaluations and improvements aside, trust your own style. Even if someone else might choose to do your job a different way, your methods may be just as effective.

■ HOME EFFICIENCY

Time management begins at home. If you're a family person, you can streamline your home life by designating one place in your home where everyone puts their important papers, thereby ensuring they don't get lost or mixed up.

Buy extra greeting cards for birthdays, thank-you, congratulations, get-well wishes, etc. so you don't have to make a special trip to the store for every occasion.

Plan your breakfast before you go to bed at night, so when you get up the next morning, you have one less thing to decide.

Of course, home life should never be reduced to a set of structured routines. Efficiency should not be the governing principle at all times, or it could squeeze all the juice and spontaneity out of your days. The purpose of streamlining your time, at work and at home, is to free up more time, and simplify your life, thus making everything easier.

Look at your possessions. Have you noticed how they take space, and how many of them need to be regularly cleaned, maintained, insured, protected, or put away? Have you got closets and drawers full of clothes you don't wear? Extra things cost money, time, and energy. I recommend a purging of your "stuff"; keep only what you really use, or what gives you pleasure. Get rid of everything else. If you're uncertain about it, get rid of it. Always err on the side of simplicity. Whenever you acquire a new item, get rid of one or two old ones. Make space in your life by asking yourself "what do I really want?"

Conclusion, Part 2

■ Know Thyself

"When a man is in earnest and knows what he is about,

his work is half done."

— MIRABEAU

Who are you and what do you want? The answers to these questions are truly the keys to "time management," in the deepest sense.

Imagine, if you will, your own obituary. What would you, ideally, like it to say about who you were and what you did in your life?

■ BRAIN FOOD

Think about it. Supposing you knew you only had a year to live.

How would your priorities change?

_____

_____

_____

How would you spend your time?

_____

_____

_____

Who would you spend your time with?

_____

_____

The answers to these questions should tell you a great deal about who you are and what's important to you.

■ YOUR LIFE GOALS

"The future belongs to those who believe in the beauty of their dreams."

— ELEANOR ROOSEVELT

Time is short. Of the 24 hours in a day, how many belong entirely to you? How can you best use your discretionary hours to create the life you want? Using your "free time" in a deliberate and well-thought-out manner will enable you to accomplish more than you might imagine is possible. This is not about driving yourself mercilessly; this is about keeping sight of where your true happiness lies.

First, you need a clear idea of your life goals. What are your greatest interests, your deepest desires—for yourself, your career, your family? Let your imagination run free. What is your *dream* in life?

DON'T FORGET YOUR DREAMS

Where would you like to be, and what would you like to be doing, ten years from now? Specifically, what would you like to have different, in your life, from the way it is now? Write the answers in the spaces below:

_____

_____

_____

_____

_____

As a rule, goals should be clear and specific. This doesn't mean they won't change over time. It's best to revisit them periodically, perhaps as often as once a month. Refine them as you go, and make sure you have written them down.

■ YOUR WORK GOALS

"I start with what I want to get out of my own life," says Jim. "Keeping that first and foremost, how can I run my business in such a way that I can achieve the things I want?"

Your work should have a connection to your overarching life goals. Do your job in a way that is consistent with your most deeply-held values. If you have integrity at your job, then your work will nourish your spirit and facilitate your life goals.

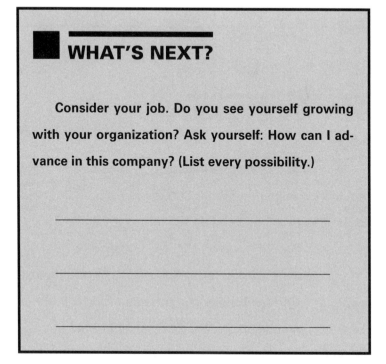

■ WHAT'S NEXT?

Consider your job. Do you see yourself growing with your organization? Ask yourself: How can I advance in this company? (List every possibility.)

_____

_____

_____

What is my best opportunity for advancement?

_____

Where can I make my most substantial contribution to the organization?

_____

What can I do in the coming days or weeks to work toward my career goals within my company?

_____

THE IDEAL JOB

Do you know what your ideal job would be? What job would best fit your aptitudes, interests, experiences, training, skill, education, and desires?

Consider your innate skills and the major accomplishments of your life. Consider your fields of interest. Now use your imagination and try to "think out of the box" as you answer the following questions:

IF NOT HERE, THEN WHERE?

What are the top three kinds of business or industries you would most like to work in? If you're already in the ideal industry, write it down.

1._____

2._____

3._____

What kinds of responsibilities would you have in your ideal job?

_____

What would be your salary in your ideal job?

_____

Would your ideal job include travel? How much?

_____

Can you name your ideal job?

_____

Career growth is a lifelong endeavor. Your idea of the perfect job will probably change. But know that you have options. If your ideal job isn't available right now, or if it doesn't even exist yet, you might still be able to create it!

■ GETTING THERE

So where do you begin? How can you realistically work toward attaining your life goals and/or your ideal job? You need a plan. Start by identifying major milestones to your goal. Those milestones are your subgoals.

Break down every subgoal into as many small steps as possible, so that you'll be able to see and measure your progress.

Make specific plans for what you intend to accomplish this year, this month, this week, this day. What can you do with your next free hour, to move you toward one of your subgoals?

Always keep your big goals in mind, no matter how small the task you're doing.

Get assistance and advice. Identify resources and people that can help you, including friends, acquaintances, professional associations, groups, seminars, classes, books, library research materials, and the internet.

Take sensible risks. Start with a few small ones and then try bigger ones. "Nothing ventured, nothing gained."

What might be a good risk for you to take in the near future, to try and bring yourself closer to one of your life goals? What do you have to lose by taking this risk? What do you have to gain? Who, besides you, might stand to lose or gain from your taking this risk?

Give yourself a reward for every subgoal you achieve.

Keep revisiting your goals. Refine and rewrite them as often as necessary. Simply keeping them in mind will prove valuable in the long run.

BALANCE

"Happiness lies not in the mere possession of money; it lies in the joy of achievement, in the thrill of creative effort."
— FRANKLIN DELANO ROOSEVELT

"One of the most tragic things I know about human nature is that all of us tend to put off living. We are all dreaming of some magical rose garden over the horizon — instead of enjoying the roses that are blooming outside our window today."
— DALE CARNEGIE

This upbeat talk about time efficiency and life goals is all well and good. But what if you wake up one morning and you feel like you can't even move?

Chances are, you've probably been pushing yourself too hard. Life is no good without relaxation and enjoyment. Use your goals to enliven and inspire yourself, not to punish or exhaust yourself.

Be reasonable about your expectations. Sometimes things take longer to accomplish than you expect. In fact, they usually do. Cut yourself some slack. As long as you are making a consistent effort to reach your goals, you will make progress. But also take regular breaks from goal-oriented purposeful activity. Enjoy the fresh air, smell the flowers, read a good book, feel the music. Release your mind. Balance is about *living* your life, not only "succeeding" in life.

"It is good to have an end to journey toward,
but it is the journey that matters, in the end."
— URSULA K. LE GUIN
(FROM *THE LEFT HAND OF DARKNESS*)

Ask yourself:

■ **Am I not enjoying my life?**

■ **Do I have a clear sense of meaning and purpose in my life?**

■ **Should I take some time off?**

Then take a slow, deep breath, close your eyes, and ask yourself:

- How am I feeling right now?

- What am I in the middle of doing right now?

- What is important in this moment?

- Make your best effort, and accept yourself as you are. That's as efficient as you can get.

■ Parting Thoughts

"The game of life is not so much in holding a good hand
as playing a poor hand well."

— H.T. LESLIE

Calvin Coolidge, 30th President of the United States said, "Nothing in the world can take the place of perseverance. Talent will not; nothing is more common than unsuccessful men with talent. Genius will not; unrewarded genius is almost a proverb. Education will not; the world is full of educated derelicts. Persistence and determination alone are omnipotent."

It has been said that in our society 3% of the people write their goals down, and 97% of the people work for the 3% that wrote down their goals. For you the happiest job in the world is the job in which you can express yourself—your interests, aptitudes, your mental and physical abilities, and natural personality—and at the same time efficiently serve your station in life.

Remember, nothing is uncovered until someone un-covers it. The better job or the better method may be hid-den; you have to discover it.

ABOUT THE AUTHOR

RONALD CLARK MENDLIN has over 40 years of ex-perience in 14 different business fields. He has received numerous commendations from government officials for project leadership and superior job performance, and has lectured extensively for community-based organizations in training of job seekers in job search methods, including lectures at the following organizations: Opportunities In-dustrialization Center West (OICW); San Mateo County Pri-vate Industry Council (PIC); Regional Occupational Program (ROP); San Quentin Pre-release Class; Twelve Step Pro-gram; Salvation Army; Western Addition Recovery House; City and County of San Francisco Day Labor Program; St. Anthony Foundation; Tenderloin Housing; San Francisco Educational Services; Ella Hill Hutch Community Center; Milestones Human Services, Inc.; San Francisco City Col-lege; San Francisco State University; Veterans' Next Step Program; Santa Clara Adult School; Sequoia Adult School.

Mr. Mendlin has helped to reorganize for maximum efficiency sections of several San Francisco City Departments, including the Board of Education, the Tax Collector's Office, the Department of Public Health, and the San Francisco Airport Commission. On a part-time work schedule, Mr. Mendlin placed directly and indirectly over 750 parolees coming out of State Prisons. Mr. Mendlin obtained jobs for residents in work furlough programs and also for residents who had 6 hours or 3 days to obtain a job or be sent back to prison. In addition he saved the San Francisco Municipal Railway from financial embarrassment in 1974. Mr. Mendlin is also the co-author of *Putting The Bars Behind You* Work Book Series (Jist Publishing Co.). These five volumes teach job search and life skills for people who recently left prison.

In addition Ronald Mendlin has:

■ Created jobs for himself at Sears, Mervyn's, Wolworth, Scofield Employment Agency and the Northern California Service League. In each case, he circumvented various employment procedures, including submitting a resume and being screened by personnel departments.

■ Been selected for civil service positions from as many as seven interviewed candidates.

■ While working at the Northern California Service League, placed hundreds of job seekers that had histories of rejection and difficulty in finding employment.

■ Attended numerous employment-related seminars and pursued extensive private study and reading on information pertaining to jobs and careers. In addition, he maintains voluminous files of information concerning jobs, careers, and management.

■ ABOUT THE CONTRIBUTORS

■ **MILT REITERMAN** rose, over 30 years, from Football Coach to Acting Superintendent of the San Francisco Unified School District. In that period of time, he held 12 Administrative Positions: Teacher; Counselor; Adult School Registrar; Curriculum Assistant; Department Head; Work Experience Program Coordinator; Supervisor of the District's Occupational Educational Program; Coordinator of Personnel Services; Assistant Superintendent of Personnel Services; Associated Superintendent of Administration (one of the top three posts under Superintendent of Schools); Deputy Superintendent; and Acting Superintendent.

When Milt retired from the San Francisco Unified

School District, he ventured into the field of Labor Relations and Negotiations. In the 22 years in this business, he served as Labor Consultant for the 1984 National Democratic Convention. In that same year, he was Labor Relations Consultant for the Moscone Convention Center and the San Francisco Housing Authority.

Milt Reiterman's achievements and contributions include taking a Superintendent's ideas and turning them into concrete action, such as his National Recruitment of Minority Teachers. He is a recipient of the St. Louise Award (Founders of the Daughters of Charity) and a Past President and Board Member of Aid Retarded Children, Inc., an agency that works with the special needs of children.

Milt has also received awards from the California Senate, including a Milt Reiterman Day. When he retired from the School District, Dianne Feinstein (then mayor, now senator from California) honored him.

■ **SHIRLEY MELNICOE** has been the Northern California Service League's Executive Director since 1986. She is a recognized authority on criminal justice — as a researcher, consultant, author, social scientist, and non-profit agency director. Her education includes a BA from UC Berkeley, and an MPA, from USC. Shirley has authored numerous publications and lectured regularly at the FBI Academy on police research. She is a past president of the Association for Criminal Justice Research.

I wish you, the reader, all success in life, business, and time management.